Getting
Acquainted
with
Accounting

Getting Acquainted with Accounting

Second Edition

John L. Carey
Former Administrative Vice President, American Institute of Certified Public Accountants, and Vice President, American Accounting Association (1968–1969)

K. Fred Skousen
Professor of Accounting; Director, Institute of Professional Accountancy, Graduate School of Management, Brigham Young University

Houghton Mifflin Company   **Boston**

Atlanta   Dallas   Geneva, Illinois
Hopewell, New Jersey   Palo Alto   London

Printed in the U.S.A.

Library of Congress Catalog Card Number: 76-10904

ISBN: 0-395-24513-3

To Joyce and Julie

J.L.C.
K.F.S.

Contents

Preface

Getting Acquainted with Accounting was originally intended, as the title indicates, to help people unfamiliar with accounting learn something about it. In the second edition, its purpose remains the same—to provide a quick look at what accounting is all about.

The book is a supplementary text designed to provide a proper perspective for students beginning their study of accounting, and can be best used at the beginning of an introductory accounting principles course. The book is aimed at freshman and sophomore students; however, it should prove useful even for those in MBA programs who have not had previous exposure to accounting. The previous edition was also used successfully in intermediate accounting courses at a number of schools.

This book does not attempt to teach accounting, but rather shows how it fits into the American economy. What is accounting? What does it do? How does it affect people's lives? How has it evolved? What is its future likely to be?

With answers to questions such as these, students of accounting should be better able to focus on the theories and the techniques. They will see how the many separate parts fit together into a useful whole and will know the *why* as well as the *what* and the *how*.

Even those students who don't intend to learn the "what" and "how" may find it helpful to gain a general idea of the nature, scope, and uses of accounting. Without some understanding of this kind, it is, for instance, difficult to read a financial statement, to grasp the basic concepts of income taxes, or to appraise the quality of financial management of a business or nonprofit organization.

Many first-year accounting textbooks begin with the rules and procedures of double-entry bookkeeping. Bookkeeping is a necessary, but only an elementary, part of accounting. Accountants must understand bookkeeping, but their work goes far beyond it. Bookkeeping presents little intellectual challenge unless the students realize how its end products are used and why they are useful.

Instead of concentrating on how to do accounting, this book tries to provide a broad overview of accounting in all its phases before the reader confronts the basic technical material. It begins with a discussion of what accounting is and how it fits into society. It then describes the evolution of accounting and discusses the relationship of accounting to all business activity. After discussing the end products of the accounting processes—accounting reports—the book concentrates on specialty areas within the accounting profession, including auditing, managerial accounting, and income tax accounting. The book concludes by discussing how accounting has attained professional status, by describing the outlook for accounting in the future, and by identifying career opportunities in the field of accountancy.

In the second edition, specific examples and illustrations of business concepts and situations have been added in order to make the book more understandable for students with non-business backgrounds. Certain portions of the book have been expanded, including a discussion of business organizations; the relationship of accounting to economics, statistics, mathematics, and other business-related subjects; the impact of accounting on various users of financial information; the role of the computer in accounting and business in today's environment; and such other current developments in accounting as the establishment of the Financial Accounting Standards Board and the increasing influence of the Securities and Exchange Commission. Similarly, certain aspects of the book have been condensed; for example, the evolutionary and historical aspects of the development of generally accepted accounting principles have been somewhat consolidated. There has been a reorganization of several sections in the early chapters—specifically, Chapters 1 through 4—to improve the logic of topic coverage and sequence. Finally, discussion questions have been added at the end of each chapter to facilitate classroom use. Guideline answers to these questions are provided at the end of the book.

As in the earlier edition, selected references are provided for those students who would like to study in greater depth some of the concepts and principles presented briefly in this book.

The reader should bear in mind that most of the topics in this book will be discussed in later accounting courses when the concepts, standards, and techniques are examined in detail. The reader should not be concerned, therefore, if everything in this book is not immediately clear. Some items will naturally be unfamiliar, and the student may find them somewhat difficult to understand at first. To repeat, the purpose here is only to convey an impression of what accounting is all about. Additional comprehension of the subject matter will follow as some of the mechanical aspects of accounting are studied. It would be particularly useful for students to review *Getting Acquainted with Accounting* periodically during their introductory accounting courses. Many accounting students have also found the book useful in explaining their chosen profession to family and friends.

The authors would like to express appreciation to the users and reviewers of the first edition, many of whom have made helpful suggestions for the book's improvement. Special thanks are due to Thomas Lenchen, Wilbur Wright College; Sue Robinson, North Harris County Community College; Roman Salazar, Modesto Junior College; and Carl Wolters, Merritt College, who reviewed the first edition. Ann Green, Bee County College; Karl Herde, Brigham Young University; and Dennis Mohn, Mount Hood Community College and Portland State College, provided particularly helpful suggestions for the second edition.

To all those who have assisted in any way in this revision, we express our gratitude. It is hoped that readers of this book will indeed be better acquainted with the profession of accounting and the role it plays in society.

J.L.C.
K.F.S.

Getting Acquainted with Accounting

1

What Is Accounting?

Accounting has been called the fastest growing profession in the United States. In the more than thirty years since 1945, the number of accountants has more than tripled. This trend still continues. Today there are over 500,000 accountants in this country, many of whom are accredited professionals. For the most part, these professionals work as independent certified public accountants (CPAs), as controllers or chief financial officers in industry, as university professors, or as executives in top-level government positions and in nonprofit organizations such as hospitals.

Why is there continued and increasing demand for accountants? What do accountants do? Why do the theory and practice of accounting have a significant impact upon the economic decisions of all members of our society? In this book, the authors attempt to answer these and similar questions. The various responsibilities and activities of accountants are explored in some detail in later chapters. This chapter deals with the nature of the accounting discipline and its relationship to society.

In today's business environment no organization can be run successfully without accounting. This is as true of the smallest organization—a bookstore, church, hospital, YMCA branch, opera company, or even a family—as it is of the largest—the United States government or General Motors. No one can manage an organization with complete success without having either sufficient knowledge of accounting or the assistance of an accountant. Indeed, no business of any size can survive in the United States without the aid of skilled accountants.

Why is this? What has cast this process called accounting, which some people mistakenly confuse with bookkeeping, into such an essential, such a pervasive role in American society?

Information for Allocation of Resources

It's really quite simple. Accounting provides a special kind of information that is absolutely necessary for the intelligent use of the resources available to any organization. No matter how rich an organization is, its resources are limited. To be sure, the richer an organization is, the more it can waste and still survive. But it cannot survive without making some intelligent decisions about how to use its resources. And it cannot make such decisions without the kind of information that accounting provides.

How is accounting used in deciding how to employ available resources? At the least complicated level, that of personal decision making, an individual or a family must decide whether to buy a house or to rent living quarters, whether to buy a television set or a car, whether to have a daughter's teeth straightened or to take the family on a vacation. Can the family safely borrow money or buy on credit? How much should they save for education of the children and for support of themselves in old age? How should they invest their savings? Sound decisions require *information*, in this case about such items as taxes, interest, insurance, rent, the costs of maintaining a house and a car, and how much income a family can reasonably expect in the future. People are faced with *choices among alternative courses of action*. If they decide without adequate information (which happens all too often), financial disaster may result.

At a higher level of complexity, the management of a business corporation is also continually confronted with choices among alternative courses of action. Should new machinery be purchased? Should a new product be launched? Should prices be raised or lowered? Should more people be hired? Should another company be absorbed? Should additional capital be acquired, and if so, by means of bank loans or by the issuance of bonds or stock? What are the probable costs and resulting revenue of each action? Sound answers to these questions require accounting information of the most sophisticated kind.

Of critical importance is the accounting information which a banker must have in deciding whether to lend money, or which investors must have in deciding whether to buy bonds or stocks. In order to make intelligent use of the resources at their disposal, they need such information to judge whether a loan is likely to be repaid or whether an investment is likely to yield a fair return.

Perhaps the highest level of complexity is required in the decisions which the federal government must make in using the immense resources that it derives from the taxation of individuals and corporations. (Incidentally, taxes are based mainly on accounting information.) The large amounts of money at the government's disposal, the scope and variety of its activities, and the difficulty of measuring the results of many of its expenditures present formidable problems to the accountants called upon to provide the policy makers with useful information. How many billions of dollars should be allocated to defense; how many billions to health, education, and welfare; and how many billions to crime prevention, protection of the environment, low-cost housing, administration of justice, and thousands of other governmental activities? Many able accountants in and out of government have been working hard for years to improve the quality of the information on which such decisions must be based. Progress is still being made.

Quality is an important word in this context. Accounting information does not consist merely of cold, impersonal masses of figures. It is a finished product, directed to specific purposes. It can be, and often is, accompanied by advice. The process by which it is derived consists of three steps: (1) collecting, classifying, and analyzing data (not only facts but also estimates and projections, when appropriate); (2) testing the data for validity (Are they reliable?) and relevance (Are they really significant for the immediate purpose?); and, (3) interpreting the data for those who will use the information (How does it affect the choices to be made?).

Information for Organizations: Internal and External

Accounting provides information for two distinct but closely related purposes: (1) making decisions within an organization and (2) reporting to persons outside the organization who have a legitimate interest in its affairs.

Every organization must both make decisions and report to outsiders. Accounting is usually identified with business, that is, with profit-making organizations. But it is equally necessary in charitable, educational, religious, governmental, and other nonprofit organizations, including membership associations of all kinds (for example, unions, trade associations, clubs). The difference is, of course, that a business must generate its own resources, and to do so it must sooner or later make profits, whereas nonprofit organizations acquire resources mainly through contributions, grants, dues, or taxes. Both, however, need information for making decisions on how to use their resources to the best advantage.

Both types of organizations also have an obligation to report to interested parties outside the organization. Businesses must file income tax returns. To borrow money from banks, they must submit financial statements. If they are incorporated, they must send similar statements to stockholders. Many businesses are regulated by governmental agencies, which also require periodic financial reports. Nonprofit organizations normally send financial reports to those who provide their funds. Some are required to do so; many others do so voluntarily to encourage continued support. A few still escape the obligation.

The uses of accounting within the organization are usually described as providing information for planning, control, and decision making. The external financial reporting function is often described as discharging accountability to those who are entitled to information about the organization's affairs.

Accounting and the Individual

Since accounting provides information for decision making, it is largely a medium of communication, and it has often been called a language. While the parallel may not be precise, there are similarities. Accountants do have a vocabulary of their own, and they have developed standards, procedures, and forms of presentation that might be compared with rules of grammar. Like a language, too, accounting is changed and refined by usage.

Business executives, government officials, and administrators of nonprofit organizations who do not have at least a general familiarity with this language must work under a severe handicap. They must rely heavily on those who do speak the language in utilizing the resources under their control and in discharging their accountability to those to whom they are responsible.

Indeed, it has often been said that no citizen can claim to be well educated who is entirely ignorant of accounting. Every cultured person in an industrial civilization should know the languages of the time. Just as it was important in earlier days to know Latin or French, so in modern times accounting is one of the languages that a person might do well to master. Accordingly, it has been suggested that introductory courses in accounting should be included not only in business school programs but also in liberal arts curricula.

It is true that it is difficult to acquire an understanding of how the American economy works without some familiarity with accounting. The nature and uses of profits, the impact of taxation, the causes of inflation, for example, are hard to grasp without any knowledge of basic accounting concepts. Citizens may unwittingly cast votes against their own interests if they are wholly ignorant of such matters. How can they vote intelligently on a school bond issue, for example, if they can't understand the school budget, which is a product of accounting?

Social Contribution of Accounting

Enough has been said, it is hoped, to demonstrate that accounting makes a significant contribution to the successful operation of all kinds of organizations. It is through these organizations that the goods and services desired by the people are provided. In facilitating the efficient management of business, governmental and nonprofit organizations—that is to say, the most effective use of their resources—accounting directly helps to raise the standard of living of all people. And without question, Americans as a whole enjoy the highest standard of living that the world has yet known.

It is true that poverty, disease, and illiteracy have not been wholly eliminated in the United States; that the industrial society has seriously polluted the environment; that some racial minorities have not enjoyed equal opportunities; and that the quality of life—cultural, aesthetic, spiritual—leaves much to be desired. Some progress is being made in tackling these problems. *But no progress can be made without a sound economic base.* Without adequate resources, wisely used and widely distributed, no nation can achieve the goals that Americans have set for themselves.

America has practically solved the production problem by developing sources of energy, by inventing or improving labor-saving machinery, and by introducing mass-production methods.

But if the wealth that is produced is concentrated in the hands of a few—a rich elite—then only that privileged class can enjoy a life of fine quality and self-fulfillment. Historically this has been the usual situation. It is the situation in some countries today, and it was to some extent true of the United States during its first hundred years.

Now the distribution of wealth in this nation is wider than ever in history; this has been achieved through income taxes, inheritance taxes, social security and unemployment insurance, government programs in housing, health, education, and welfare, and the activities of private organizations directed to the same ends. Legislation strengthening the bargaining power of unions has increased labor's share of the fruits of production. Regulatory agencies protect the consumer against monopolistic prices. And emerging movements to combat pollution, to eliminate disease, and to provide equal opportunities for disadvantaged minorities are making headway.

Production of sufficient goods and services has been made possible only through the accumulation of large amounts of money—capital—by channeling the savings of millions of people into large industrial enterprises. The capital is used to provide sources of energy—coal, oil, gas, electricity—and to buy the plants and machinery necessary for mass production.

But people won't invest their savings without adequate information, and this need is met largely through financial reports provided by accountants.

The widespread distribution of wealth among the people is accomplished largely through the tax system, which skims off large amounts of business profits and individual incomes and redistributes them in the form of financial aids and countless services. This tax system could not exist without accounting, through which profits and incomes are determined.

Exploitation of labor, consumers, investors, and other segments of the population is discouraged by a profusion of laws, administered by a network of governmental agencies. Almost all of these agencies require accounting information in order to determine whether or not violations have occurred.

None of these systems works perfectly, of course. In human affairs perfection is elusive. But the combined activities of business, government, and private nonprofit organizations have worked well enough to give Americans as a whole a greater degree of security, a wider range of opportunities, and a wider variety of choices than any other population has enjoyed.

Information for the Allocation of Resources to Social Goals

There is a danger, however, that impatience for more rapid progress may overstrain even the abundant resources of the United States. A nation can spend itself into bankruptcy or into an inflationary spiral that could wreck its economy. Resources, however great, are always limited. It is impossible to do everything at once to as great an extent as everyone desires.

This does not mean that hopes must be deferred or that efforts to expedite progress must be retarded. What it does mean is that resources must be allocated in a way that will do the most good at the least cost.

The problem—and the opportunity—for accounting in the years ahead is to provide information that will facilitate choices among various programs—all of which may be good—in relation to the amount of resources they would consume and the resources or benefits they would provide. This is known as a cost-benefit relationship.

Conducting a cost-benefit analysis presents no insuperable difficulties when the probable benefits are sufficiently tangible to be expressed in terms of money, as in the production and sale of familiar goods and services. The difficulties are formidable, however, when the benefits cannot be measured, as the costs are measured, in terms of money. Dollar signs cannot be affixed to proposed improvements in the quality of life. For example, to what extent, if any, should government use tax money to subsidize opera, ballet, or theater? The answer depends on subjective judgment in the absense of an ability to measure the expected benefits in relation to the cost. Should every American youth be entitled to a free college education? What kind of education? What benefits would it produce for the individuals concerned or for society? Would it be worth the cost to the taxpayers?

Similar questions arise with respect to universal health care, governmental subsidies of low-cost housing, rehabilitation of drug addicts and criminals, pollution control, and countless other desirable social goals.

The objectives would attract almost unanimous support if the nation's resources were unlimited, but they are not. Choices must be made, priorities must be determined. And this requires information of the kind that accounting provides. Some accountants have been working on problems of this nature, and more will be doing so. Future possibilities are discussed in Chapter 9.

Summary

This chapter has attempted to provide a bird's-eye view of the nature and scope of accounting, and the way accounting fits into the economic environment. In following chapters accounting's various uses will be explored in somewhat greater detail.

In brief, accounting is utilitarian in nature. That is, accounting provides quantitative information useful for making economic decisions. To the extent that accounting fulfills its role in providing relevant and reliable information, better decisions are possible and scarce resources are utilized more efficiently. This will result in an increased standard of living for all members of society.

Later chapters will explore current and future opportunities of the accounting profession. At this point it is sufficient to bear in mind that accounting is essential to the efficient management of all organizations, that it has significant impact on the lives of people, and that it pervades the entire structure of an industrial society, from the highest levels of government to the individual family. Furthermore, it will be seen that its development to present levels is comparatively recent and that it is now on the threshold of wider opportunities for service.

Discussion Questions

1   What is the primary purpose of accounting?

2   How does accounting contribute to the welfare of a society?

3   How is a knowledge of accounting beneficial to nonaccountants?

4   As an investor, how would your viewpoint of accounting's role differ from a manager's viewpoint?

5   If accounting is so essential and pervasive in our society, why has its rapid development to present levels been so recent?

2
Evolution of Accounting

Accounting is the product of its environment. Hermits do not need accounting; organizations of people do. It has evolved, as have law, medicine, and other fields of human activity, in response to the economic and social needs of people living together in organized groups.

The present scope of accounting embraces most of the information needed by managers of organizations for both internal and external reporting purposes. The scope of accounting is far broader today than it was even fifty years ago—to say nothing of preindustrial times—and it continues to expand. This is because accounting must respond to changing needs in an ever more complex economic and social environment. This environment has also responded to advances in accounting, since the availability of sophisticated accounting techniques has made possible economic transactions and social programs that otherwise could not have been undertaken successfully.

The history of accounting and its interactions with evolving economic systems is a fascinating study in itself. It throws light on how people made their living and how whole nations improved their economic positions. For the present purposes, however, it is necessary only to understand, in a general way, how accounting developed to the place it is today.

Primitive Accounting

Ever since people have lived in organized social groups, they have kept track of their affairs by keeping records of some kind, in very early times by marks on stone or clay. Archaeologists have dug up records of tax collections and simple transactions in the ruins of ancient Sumeria and Egypt, which are believed to have been the earliest civilizations.

Commerce is as old as civilization. The ancient Phoenicians and the Greeks, both sea-going people, were great traders who developed currencies and banking systems to facilitate the activities of their merchants. Accounting records and reports inevitably accompanied these activities.

Masters who entrusted slaves or servants with the management of goods or properties naturally required financial reports of their stewardship. *Agency accounting* is a term applied to such reporting.

Double-Entry Bookkeeping

It was not until 1494, however, that the idea of double-entry bookkeeping was presented to the world in a published treatise by an Italian monk named Luca Pacioli. The ideas presented in his treatise were no doubt based on practices which others had evolved over long periods of time.

This was a milestone. Double-entry bookkeeping has been called a monumental discovery. Using double-entry bookkeeping, for the first time a business was able to keep a complete and coordinated record of all its transactions, and ultimately to draw from this record the integrated financial statements now in common use. The enormous advantage that this system provided over earlier record-keeping procedures was the ability to see at once the profit or loss for a given time period (month, year, voyage) and the related assets, liabilities, and *net worth* (now called *equity*) of the owner or owners of the enterprise.

The availability of new techniques encouraged large-scale enterprises. The resources of a number of people could be pooled to finance a single venture, like the voyage of a merchant ship, and the profits could be divided equitably among the participants on the basis of the financial statements.

Such isolated ventures were gradually replaced by continuing business organizations, in which the initial capital contributed by participants (partners) could be augmented, if desired, by reinvesting a portion of the profits.

The Corporation

Arrangements of this sort led naturally to the conception of the corporation, which was first legally established in England in 1845. This, in turn, immediately stimulated the development of new accounting practices.

The corporation, of course, is a creature of the law, an "artificial person." Those who organize it are permitted to sell shares of ownership—stock—to anyone who cares to invest. The fact that the legal liability of stockholders is limited is an attractive feature: They may lose their investment capital, but they have no further liability, as individuals or partners do. Also, stockholders may sell their shares quickly, usually on the open market.

However, stockholders normally hope for a return on their investment in the form of dividends, a share of the profits. They also hope that if the corporation is highly profitable, the value of their shares will increase, and that these shares can then be sold to produce a capital gain.

The Industrial Revolution, which began in England in the mid-eighteenth century, resulted in demands for massive amounts of capital to build plants and buy machinery. The corporate form of organization facilitated the accumulation of this needed capital from a large number of individual shareholders, each contributing a relatively small amount. This practice, however, created a class of owners who could not participate actively in the management of the business. The law recognized that their rights must be protected. One form of protection was a requirement in the English law that the management submit to stockholders periodic financial statements showing the company's financial position and, later, the profit or loss for a certain period, usually a year.

Financial statements were also offered to potential investors who might wish to purchase stock. In the course of time such statements were included in the *prospectus*, a statement describing the company and its operations, which accompanied an offer to sell shares.

Thus, by the beginning of the twentieth century, accounting had ceased to serve only the private function between master and servant, owner and employee, or partner and partner. More of the world's work was done by corporations.

The number of stockholders who were also voters increased rapidly. Corporate accounting was becoming a matter of high-level economic, social, and political concern.

Industrialization of the United States

In the United States, the development of accounting has followed close upon the growth of an industrial nation. From the time of securing its independence to the time of the Civil War, the United States was predominantly an agricultural country. The population was mostly rural. The principal sources of energy were wind, water, animals, and human labor.

But sustained industrialization was beginning. The Industrial Revolution spread rapidly to the United States. The use of machinery and steam power greatly increased productivity, and new inventions appeared in rapid succession.

After the Civil War the United States rapidly became one of the leading industrial nations. Railroads were built and factories mushroomed. Electricity and petroleum were developed as sources of energy.

At the turn of the century the automobile was invented, soon followed by the airplane. Whole new industries sprang up based on new inventions like motion pictures, radio, television, computers, to name a few highly visible ones.

Capital Formation and Financial Reporting

As in England, large infusions of capital were necessary to start new ventures; for example, in manufacturing, mining, transportation, and electric power industries. And, as in England, the corporation was the most convenient form of organization for this purpose.

While there was as yet no law in the United States requiring it, most corporations, in order to provide assurance to investors and creditors, issued periodic financial statements showing their financial positions and the results of operation. These financial statements will be described in Chapter 4.

However, there was room for a good deal of flexibility in financial reporting in the early days. So rapid had been the

process of industrialization and the widespread distribution
of corporate securities to the public, that no authoritative
standards of financial reporting had been developed to which
all companies had to conform. Some companies submitted
complete reports while a few took advantage of their free-
dom to omit disclosures that would cast an unfavorable light
on their performance. The opportunity for subjective judgment was much wider than it is now. Inevitably, some misleading financial reports were issued, and investors suffered
losses as a consequence.

Since then great progress has been made. Steps were
taken by the accounting profession, the stock exchanges, and
the Securities and Exchange Commission to formulate accounting standards and disclosure requirements that must be
followed. As a result, financial statements have become vastly
more informative than they were forty years ago.

Progress in this area is still being made and will no doubt
continue. The improvement of financial reporting has for
many years been a major project of the accounting profession
and of others concerned. As the number of stockholders
increases, the importance of accounting in the process of capital formation in a free-enterprise economy cannot be overem-
phasized. The continued improvement of financial reporting
is a vivid example of response to social change.

Scientific Management

In addition to information needed to discharge accountability to investors and creditors, the burgeoning American
business enterprises needed increasing amounts of timely and
relevant information for planning, control, and decision making within their own organizations.

In earlier days businesses were more or less isolated geo-
graphically and were smaller and less complex. Competition
was not so keen. Business executives were less sophisticated.
Accounting was relatively primitive. In these circumstances
plans and decisions were often based on the subjective judgment of individual owners or executives, guided by intuition
or hunch. An inelegant expression used to describe such intu-
itive decisions was "flying by the seat of the pants."

But as improved transportation and communications intensified competition among far-flung enterprises, the managers who relied on complete information indicating the probable consequences of alternative choices proved to have an overwhelming advantage.

Early in the twentieth century a movement known as *scientific management* began to attract attention. Its proponents stressed a systematic approach to the solution of management problems, based on hard information.

Accountants were quick to get involved in scientific management. In the United States they had already made a good deal of headway in the field of cost accounting. During World War I government contracts for the supply of war materials were based largely on costs. This stimulated the interest of business executives in more precisely analyzing the various elements of cost and their interrelations than had formerly been customary. Cost control and cost analysis are obviously significant functions in all aspects of planning and decision making. Rapidly the field of accounting expanded to embrace the development of information to aid in the solution of business problems of many kinds.

The advent of computers greatly accelerated this trend. Systematic analysis of complex business operations naturally requires the accumulation of adequate and timely data related to these operations. The computer makes it possible to store and manipulate data on a scale unattainable by manual means. Computer technology has resulted in the development of vast quantities of data in large corporations as well as in government, and also in the design of information systems that facilitate the extraction and rearrangement of the data for various specific purposes.

As will be shown later, modern accounting has embraced these activities in response to changing social needs.

Governmental Regulation of Business

As happens in all human affairs, abuses crept into the practices of some corporations. For example, a company with great resources could cut prices to drive out smaller competitors in the industry, could fix prices by agreement with competitors, or could buy up competing companies so as to control the market and then charge the highest prices the traffic would bear. To prevent such restraints on competition, the antitrust laws were enacted.

Some industries, however, like electric utilities, are "natural" monopolies. When one such utility (with its large capital investment of plant and equipment) already exists in a given area, it would seem foolish to go to the enormous expense of building another. To prevent companies in these industries from exploiting the public, laws were enacted to limit their rates (prices) to amounts yielding profits considered to be a fair return on invested capital. This rate-making process requires extensive accounting information.

The banks and insurance companies to which the people entrust their savings also came under legal regulation, involving record-keeping and reporting requirements and periodic examination of their accounts.

Later, laws were passed to regulate the activities of stock exchanges, stockbrokers, and investment companies. These laws also involved accounting and financial reporting requirements.

These are only a few examples of governmental regulatory activities that could not have been effective if accounting had not developed to a point at which the necessary information could be provided.

Social Programs of Government

As the growing industrial economy vastly increased the production of wealth, the gap between the rich and the poor tended to widen. The mass of the people pressed for a more equitable distribution of the pie.

The income tax law enacted in 1913 was an initial step in that direction. Together with inheritance taxes, it slowed down the accumulation of huge personal fortunes and provided the government with a rich source of revenue available for social services.

The income tax was a tremendous stimulus to accounting. Every corporation, every small business, and every individual who enjoyed more than minimal income was forced to keep

good records to serve as supporting evidence of the amount
of tax paid and to avoid overpaying the tax. And the complexities involved in determining business income led to urgent
demands for the advice and assistance of trained accountants.

Social Security and Medicare are two other programs of
incredible magnitude, involving the collection of taxes and
contributions in relatively small amounts from tens of millions
of individuals and the distribution of billions of dollars, again
in relatively small amounts, for old-age assistance and medical
care. In the case of Medicare, hospital costs attributable to
insured patients, and therefore to be reimbursed by the government, also must be checked by examination of hospital
accounting records to guard against error or fraud. The scope
and complexity of accounting systems and functions involved
in Social Security and Medicare are awesome.

In addition to these programs, the government makes
grants of funds for research and education, for construction
of housing for low-income citizens and of hospitals for war
veterans, and for many other purposes. In each instance an
effort is made, through accounting procedures, to ensure that
the money is spent for the intended purposes and that the
costs are reasonable.

The programs described here by no means exhaust the
list of governmental social programs and services. No mention
has been made, for example, of welfare and unemployment
insurance. Not only the federal government but also state and
local governments are involved in similar programs, all of
which require accounting information as a basis for financial
control.

The present discussion is intended only to illustrate the
various ways in which government has gradually intervened
in the economy, taken on social services that previously were
left to private charities, and entered into innumerable transactions with individual citizens and with private businesses, all
involving use of accounting information.

Internal Accounting of Government
The far-flung accounting activities of the governmental
agencies and related organizations, developing as they did

gradually over a long period of time, inevitably led to some duplication, inefficiency, and waste. Some overall, centralized control was essential. In 1921 legislation was passed creating the Bureau of the Budget and the General Accounting Office to provide such control.

In 1948 these agencies, with the Treasury Department, launched a Joint Financial Management Improvement Program with the objective of coordinating budgeting, accounting, auditing, and other financial management functions in the operations of the federal government as a whole.

Keeping track of the billions of dollars handled by the government, measuring results against costs, minimizing waste and inefficiency, and guarding against errors and fraud constitute an accounting problem of gigantic proportions. Tens of thousands of accountants are employed in the task, which is a never-ending one.

Small Business Accounting
A major portion of the private business activity of the United States is conducted by giant corporations whose securities are issued to the public and traded in the capital markets. Their financial reports are of immediate concern to tens of millions of investors. Naturally, the efforts to refine accounting principles underlying such reports have been concentrated on the problems of big business.

But there are millions of smaller business enterprises conducting commercial and industrial activities in America. These small businesses are naturally more numerous in industries that do not require heavy capital investment, as steel production and automobile manufacturing do, for example. Research-oriented industries, as in the electronics field, and service businesses, like small banks, retail shops, restaurants, motels, and recreational facilities, predominate among the smaller enterprises.

Small enterprises usually do not have access to as wide a range of expert advice as is available to large corporations. It is frequently the accountant who brings to the small business the ability to provide information needed both for internal management and external reporting purposes. The accountant can adapt the principles and techniques that have proven successful in large organizations to meet the particular needs of a smaller one.

Accounting in Nonprofit Organizations

There are countless national, regional, and local organizations devoted to charitable, scientific, educational, political, mutual improvement, social, and other purposes. In the aggregate they handle billions of dollars derived from dues, fees, grants, contributions, and the sale of publications or services. They constitute an important segment of the economy, and any serious attempt at allocation of national resources has to take them into account.

Since their objectives are not to make profits, but to accomplish purposes that are not readily translatable into dollars, it is usually difficult to judge how effectively they allocate the resources utilized. As suggested earlier, the same problem confronts governmental units.

Reference was made in Chapter 1 to the challenge now facing accountants to develop techniques for measuring the cost-benefits relations in nonprofit activities. Without such information it seems impossible to make a rational determination of priorities.

Accountants have done some pioneering in this area, but much remains to be done. Meanwhile, the nonprofit organizations, for the most part, follow internal accounting and financial reporting patterns adapted from those in the business world, which are not wholly satisfactory for nonprofit enterprises.

Accounting and Economic Controls

American society has been called pluralistic—it is composed of so many disparate elements that it defies a generalized definition. The difficulty of describing it is compounded by the rapidity with which it has changed in a short time span, equivalent to the lifetimes of three individuals.

Yet under the swirling surface of diverse activities strong currents flowing toward specific objectives can be detected.

The first and most essential objective—elimination of extreme poverty—has almost been reached. Meanwhile, much progress has been made toward improvement of health care, education, opportunities for recreation—elements of a better quality of life. Indeed, so much progress has been made that many people, having seen what can be done, are demanding more, better, and faster. The strain on the nation's resources has become evident. More and more of these resources are under direct or indirect control of government—in the so-called public sector—rather than in the hands of private organizations.

As government exercises increasing control over economic activities, it must depend on accounting information in making plans and formulating broad policies. Through its control of interest rates, the supply of money in circulation, and the volume of its own expenditures, the government can stimulate business activity or retard it. Through special provisions in the income tax law, government can encourage certain kinds of economic or social behavior, such as accelerated investment in new machinery or private contributions to educational, charitable, and religious organizations.

In order to make intelligent decisions on matters of such vital importance to all citizens, reliable information is essential on business profits, sales, volume of employment, wage scales, consumer purchases, capital investment, changes in price levels, and many other matters. Many of the source data are provided by accountants from the information systems of the individual enterprises that make up the total economy. And the classification of the data, their testing for validity and relevance, and the interpretation of the resulting information constitute accounting functions—even though until now they have been carried on mainly by economists and statisticians in government.

An overview of the economic results of the nation's activities as a whole is also essential to policy makers at the highest level. In preparing the federal budget it is necessary, for example, to estimate revenues from taxation, which depend heavily on business profits and on salaries and wages paid to employees. Trends in the economy on which these and other estimates can be based in part are reflected in national income accounts, the annual gross national product

figure, and the international balance of payments accounts.
Accounting concepts and procedures are used in the production of these informative guides.

The complexities involved in gathering, analyzing, and
interpreting the data necessary to provide an overview of an
entire nation's economy truly stagger the imagination. Accountants have much to contribute to improvement of the
process, as a basis for better decision making by government.

Opportunities for additional contributions present themselves in the growing need for better allocation of the nation's
strained resources in accordance with determined priorities.
The possibilities will be discussed in Chapter 9, which deals
with the future of accounting.

Summary

From the most primitive record keeping at the dawn of
civilization, accounting has developed into a provider of essential information in the highly complex American society.
Indeed, it is not too much to say that this pluralistic society
could not survive in its present structure without the information accounting provides.

Through the centuries accounting has been adopted,
refined, and expanded to meet the needs of the contemporary society. In turn, society has reacted to the availability of
improved accounting concepts and methods by venturing into more complicated areas of economic activity.

Following the Industrial Revolution and the development of the corporation, financial accounting became a matter of vital interest to a rapidly increasing number of people
who invested their savings in corporate securities.

As American business became increasingly competitive
and complex, new approaches to efficient management were
based on accounting information.

As government intervened more and more in the economy and responded to public demand for various social programs, accounting provided the information necessary for
effective regulation of business and management of public
funds.

Now accounting is faced with yet another problem, the

development of information on which decisions can be made about the relative costs and benefits of programs whose results cannot be measured in terms of dollars.

While accommodating all these diverse needs, however, the basic concepts of accounting have endured. They have provided a continuity of information which has been a stabilizing force, helping orderly transition from one stage of economic development to another.

Discussion Questions

1   Why was the invention of double-entry bookkeeping important?

2   Why did the Industrial Revolution stimulate the formation of corporations and, therefore, accounting?

3   Why did the role of accounting increase with the emergence of the corporation?

4   Why did the development of scientific management require greater accounting skills?

5   Why has the increased role of government in society called for more accountants?

6   What are some significant differences between accounting for business enterprises and accounting for nonprofit organizations?

3

Impact of Business Activity upon Accounting

The term *business* in the broadest sense is used to identify the production and distribution of all goods and services on which a nation's standard of living—and therefore the quality of life enjoyed by its people—depends. In the United States most business is conducted by private organizations which must make a profit to survive. However, some business is carried on by governmental and other nonprofit organizations subsidized in one way or another by government grants or private donations.

A major function of accounting is to measure the results of business activity. The previous chapter described how accounting has evolved to meet the changing needs of business environments. The purpose of this chapter is to describe briefly the general nature of business, to show the relationship of accounting to business, and to identify the various uses of accounting as it helps efficient conduct of the basic business activities. Hopefully, this will help the student better visualize the interdisciplinary relationships of accounting with finance, production, marketing, economics, and other business-related topics. This chapter also discusses the development of accounting principles and the influence upon that development, and therefore on society as a whole, of various professional groups, such as the Financial Accounting Standards Board, the Accounting Principles Boards, and the Securities and Exchange Commission.

Business Activity

Businesses take many forms. A business may be owned and operated by a single individual (a proprietorship), or by a small group of individuals (a partnership), or by several or many stockholders (a corporation). A business may manufacture goods, may sell finished goods, or may provide services rather than goods. A business may be a small, local establishment or a large multinational company. Regardless of the type of business, its product, its organizational form, or its size and complexity, there are some common elements of business activity.

Every business must have a reason for its existence. For all profit-oriented businesses, a primary objective is to provide goods or services to others at a price that will cover the costs of producing the product or service and return an additional amount (profit) to the owners of the business. This profit motive is an essential ingredient in America's free-enterprise system.

For a nonprofit institution, for example, a university or a hospital, the primary objective is not to make a profit but to provide services consistent with the charter and objectives of the institution in an efficient manner.

In accomplishing their objectives, organizations, whether profit oriented or not, must first acquire the resources needed to carry on their activities. The resources initially come from investments by owners, loans from creditors, or in some instances gifts or appropriations from foundations or from city, state, or national government agencies. The resources are the *assets* of the business and the claims against those assets are the *liabilities* and *owners' equities*. (The accounting equation—Assets = Liabilities + Owners' Equity—will be explained further in the next chapter.)

Money resources acquired are used to purchase other physical and service resources, for example, buildings, equipment, materials, supplies, and labor. All of these resources are utilized in producing and marketing the firm's products. As the assets are used up, they become *expenses* of the business. The expenses must be matched with *revenues* received from customers for purchases of the company's products or services in order to find out whether the company is making or losing money. If revenues exceed expenses, the result is *income* or *profit*. The profits can then be used to pay off loans (a return to creditors); to pay dividends (a return to owners); or, by retaining the profits in the business, to purchase additional materials, equipment, labor, etc., as the business once again begins its operating cycle. These interrelationships are diagrammed in Figure 1.

Most business students are required to take courses in finance, production, marketing, economics, and accounting. Figure 1 highlights these various subdivisions of business activity. Finance is concerned with acquiring the necessary funds to operate a business. As illustrated, funds may be generated internally, from profits which are retained for use in the business, or externally, by borrowing or by seeking investment capital. Production requires conversion of monetary resources into physical and service resources and eventually into the product to be sold. Marketing is the process of selling the product which, of course, is critical to the successful operation of a business. Economics has an important relationship to business in the sense that all business activity is predicated on the idea that resources are always limited and must

Figure 1   Summary of Business Activity

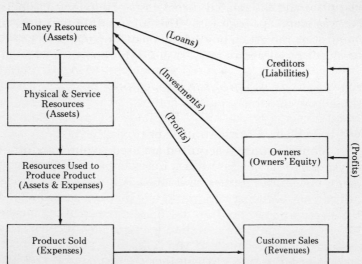

be allocated among competing alternative uses, and on the related concept of supply and demand. The relationship of supply and demand is especially significant in terms of pricing decisions. Accounting relates to each of these other disciplines because it measures and communicates information about each field of activity as well as about the results of the business as a whole.

The Accounting Process

As a business acquires resources, converts them to goods or services, and sells the firm's product, it enters into transactions with other groups. The accounting process records these transactions, summarizes them, and eventually produces financial reports that can be used to analyze and interpret the activity of a business.

The results of the accounting process are the various accounting reports needed by particular users. Figure 2 indicates various audiences who require accounting reports.

The form, content, and timing of internal accounting reports are determined by the individual needs and desires of management. For example, a plant manager may request a weekly report of the number of items produced in a particular plant and the related direct costs of production, including waste and spoilage loss. This information will help in monitoring the efficiency of the plant's operations. The vice president of sales may request monthly reports on the sales

Figure 2   Results of the Accounting Process

Internal Management Reports

Income Tax Forms Involving Most Citizens ← Accounting Process → Special Reports for Regulatory Agencies, e.g., SEC, FTC, etc.

External Financial Statements for Creditors and Investors

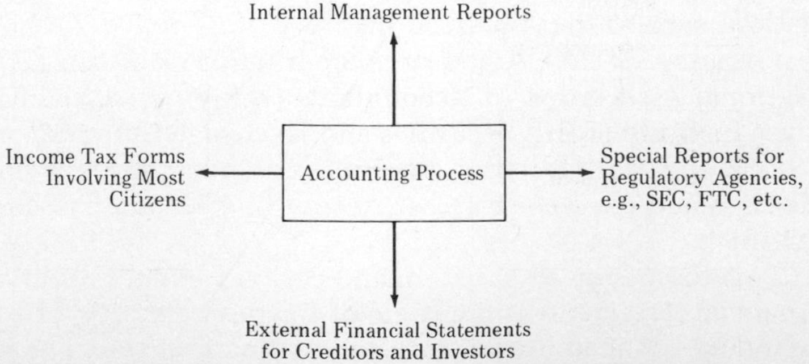

productivity and contribution to profit of each major division within the company. A division manager may need a special report analyzing the effects of dropping or adding a particular product line.

The examples described above are intended merely to be illustrative. There are many other possible examples of internal accounting reports because managers need many kinds of specific information as they operate their businesses. The main point is that one primary function of accounting is to assist management in running its business by providing relevant and timely information in the form of internal reports. The role of the managerial accountant is discussed further in Chapter 4.

Special reports required by such regulatory agencies as the Securities and Exchange Commission (SEC) or the Federal Trade Commission (FTC) must include the information specified by the applicable rules and regulations. This is, of course, also true of tax returns filed annually with the Internal Revenue Service (IRS). (Chapter 7 discusses aspects of income tax accounting.) The accounting system must be sufficiently flexible and comprehensive to produce the needed information in the format required. Satisfying regulatory reporting requirements is another important function of accounting.

High among the essential products of accounting are the general-purpose financial statements prepared for external user groups such as creditors and investors. These statements are based on "generally accepted accounting principles." The development of these principles has evolved through the years and is an ongoing process involving several important organizations such as the American Institute of Certified Public Accountants (AICPA), American Accounting Association (AAA), National Association of Accountants (NAA), Financial Executives Institute (FEI), Securities and Exchange Commission (SEC), and more recently, the Financial Accounting Standards Board (FASB) and Cost Accounting Standards Board (CASB).

A discussion of the form and content of the external financial statements is the topic of the next chapter. The role of independent auditors in attesting to financial statements is presented in Chapter 5. The remainder of this chapter will examine the development of accounting principles upon which the financial statements are based.

Development of Accounting Principles

Roughly one hundred years ago accounting's principal responsibility was to produce balance sheets providing a correct view of the state of companies' affairs as shown by the books of the companies. But at first there were no guidelines indicating how the books should be kept and how the many decisions involving estimates and judgments should be made. The quality of the accounting depended on the common sense and the personal integrity of those responsible for it.

Gradually an accounting literature developed. The practices of the prominent companies and the respected public accountants (see Chapters 5 and 8) were imitated by others who wished to do a good job. In the United States, however, where there was no national corporation law, there was room for excessive optimism, and even deliberate deception, in financial reporting. There were no authoritative, well-defined accounting principles nor standards of disclosure to which all companies were expected to conform.

Spurred in part by criticism from outside observers and in part by the exhortations of its own far-sighted leaders, the accounting profession in the mid-1920s began to establish a relation with the New York Stock Exchange that led to the issuance of the first authoritative statement of accounting principles.

Agreements with the Stock Exchange

The Exchange had power to set standards for reports to stockholders issued by companies whose shares were listed for trading on the Exchange. The organizations representing the independent auditors (see Chapter 5) and the controllers of large corporations worked out an agreement with Exchange officials on five "broad principles of accounting," which presumably were designed to close the most obvious loopholes in contemporary accounting practice. In retrospect, the five broad principles promulgated in 1934 seem primitive—they have even been called "quaint"—but they marked the beginning of a movement of historical importance.

Even more important than the statement of specific principles was the agreement on several basic concepts underlying corporate financial reporting in general. The participants concluded that a detailed set of rules binding on all corporations of a given class was utterly impracticable, in view of the wide diversity of conditions that could affect the accounting of individual corporations. Instead it was concluded that companies should be permitted to choose their own accounting methods "within reasonable limits" but must disclose their methods and use them consistently from year to year. This disclosure requirement was not implemented until 1972, but the consistency requirement, which was enforced from 1934 on, was a great step forward.

There were, and to some extent still are, alternative acceptable methods, all perfectly logical, of accounting for depreciation, inventories, income taxes, intangible assets, and many transactions peculiar to certain industries.

The rationale underlying the 1934 agreement was that consistency in the application of any acceptable method would permit valid comparisons of a single company's results for different years—in other words, earnings trends could be discerned—and over a period of time any sound method would produce substantially the same aggregate results.

The documentation supporting this 1934 agreement also established formally and publicly the concept of "accepted accounting principles" as the criterion in accordance with which the fairness of the financial statements would be judged. What those accepted principles were, in addition to the five then agreed upon, remained to be determined, and their reduction to authoritative written form has proved to be a never-ending task.

The main points covered in the agreement with the Exchange have long since been taken for granted. But at that time they marked important changes in the status quo. They affected the interests of corporate management and of investors, as well as those of the accountants and of the Exchange itself. Naturally, the negotiations had proceeded with deliberation over a period of years. Meanwhile, the stock market crash of 1929 had occurred, a new administration had assumed office in Washington, and the Securities Act of 1933 had been enacted.

The Securities Acts

The Securities Act of 1933, first known as the "Truth in Securities Bill," dealt largely with the information required to be furnished to prospective investors. It gave the government discretionary power to prescribe the form and content of the required financial statements and also the accounting methods to be followed.

A year later in 1934, a companion law, entitled the Securities Exchange Act, was enacted. Among other things, it required annual financial statements to be filed by registrants. It also created the Securities and Exchange Commission (commonly referred to as the SEC) to administer both the 1933 and 1934 acts. The SEC decided to require independent audits of the financial statements filed with it, as the law empowered it to do.

The professional accounting organizations immediately offered their cooperation to the SEC in working out forms, procedures, and regulations related to the accounting and auditing provisions of the statutes. The offer was accepted, and valuable assistance from the accountants was acknowledged.

At first there was a possibility that the SEC might exercise its authority to prescribe accounting principles and methods, but it decided, at least for the time being, not to do so. Rather, it invited the accounting profession to propose improvements in financial reporting, which the SEC, if it agreed, could impose on corporations subject to its jurisdiction by exercising its statutory authority. Continuing cooperative relations between the SEC and the professional accounting organizations were established.

It was not long, however, before representatives of the SEC began to criticize accountants for failure to eliminate what the commission considered undesirable accounting practices and for permitting too much diversity among what were regarded as "generally accepted accounting principles." In addition, within the profession itself, from both the practicing and academic branches, there was increasing pressure for an organized, purposeful approach to the development of accounting principles.

The Committee on Accounting Procedure
As a result, in 1938, the national professional society of certified public accountants (see Chapter 8) formed a Committee on Accounting Procedure, supported for the first time by a paid research staff. The committee represented a cross section of the accounting profession, including several prominent professors. The committee's charge was to narrow the areas of difference in financial reporting by encouraging elimination of less desirable practices, even though they might have been considered acceptable in the past. The committee's procedure was to publish Accounting Research Bulletins on specific topics. The conclusions of the bulletins were not binding; their authority rested on the general acceptability of the opinions, but the burden of justifying departures from the recommendations fell on those who adopted other methods.

While this approach was permissive rather than prescriptive, the result was gradual improvement in corporate financial reporting. The SEC generally required that registrants follow the committee's recommendations. Over a period of twenty-one years, fifty-one Accounting Research Bulletins were issued, indicating preferred practices in many different areas. In 1959, for reasons to be explained shortly, the Committee on Accounting Procedure was succeeded by the Accounting Principles Board.

The Changing Economic Environment
Between 1939 and 1959, there had been radical changes in the economic environment. The end of World War II in 1945 marked the beginning of an economic boom. Technological advances accelerated. New industries were launched. Old products were improved. Employment reached unprecedented levels. Social services were expanded. Consumer spending increased rapidly. Business needed large amounts of additional capital. The most convenient way to raise capital was to attract the savings of the people directly through the

sale of common stock—*equity capital.* Under the banner of
"people's capitalism" the stock exchanges actively encouraged investment in stocks by individuals. The result was a
significant increase in the number of common stockholders
from a few million to nearly 15 million. (The number is now
closer to 50 million.) In one way or another, a substantial
proportion of the American population developed a direct
or indirect financial interest in the prices of common stocks,
which depended to a large extent on the reported earnings
of the companies concerned. Accountants, who assumed responsibility for the "fairness" of reported earnings, found
themselves the objects of unaccustomed attention from the
financial press, investment analysts and advisers, federal governmental agencies and officials, including members of Congress, and particularly the SEC.

Gradually the financial community became aware that
there were alternative accounting principles on which the reporting of similar transactions could be based, so that amounts
of earnings reported by two or more companies in similar circumstances might differ solely because of differences in accounting methods. There was mounting criticism of the
independent auditors who permitted such differences and a
rising demand for "uniform accounting," which would permit valid comparisons of the earnings per share of different
companies—an impossible goal, as will be shown later, but
something had to be done.

The Accounting Principles Board

The American Institute of Certified Public Accountants,
which had created the Committee on Accounting Procedure,
replaced it in 1959 with the Accounting Principles Board,
composed of CPAs engaged in independent auditing, accounting professors, and financial executives of corporations. Its
procedures were more formal than those of the predecessor
committee. It had the support of an enlarged research division
and also consulted more widely with other interested groups,
such as corporate managements, accounting teachers, financial analysts, bankers, the stock exchanges, and the SEC.

However, members of the board differed strongly in
their views of what should be done about the demand for

uniform accounting and comparability of earnings per share. The members knew that imposition of a uniform accounting system on all companies—even on all companies in one industry—could conceal important differences in the actual factual situations to the detriment of investors, as had happened, for instance, in the case of regulated railroads.

All recognized also that a single figure of earnings per share could never be a valid guide to sound investment. For one thing, earnings per share is inevitably a distillation, in part, of estimates and judgments of future probabilities. Accounting must deal as best it can with the uncertainties that are a part of business life. One accountant declared that a single figure of corporate net income for such a short period as a year would be "indefensible if it weren't indispensable."

It was also recognized that no matter how uniform accounting principles might become, earnings per share could be raised, for example, by curtailing expenditures for advertising or research or executive development or many other purposes to the ultimate detriment of the company and its stockholders. On the other hand, desirable expenditures of this nature would reduce earnings and perhaps discourage purchase of the stock by investors who looked only at the final earnings figure.

Yet the majority of the board felt that unnecessary obstacles to comparability of earnings of different companies, arising only from differences in accounting and not reflecting differences in actual circumstances, should be eliminated. The ultimate decision was embodied in a statement of the board's objective: *Variations in treatment of accounting items generally should be confined to those justified by substantial differences in factual circumstances.* Thus, if two companies were accounting for identical transactions in identical circumstances, the same accounting principle should be followed by both. This, of course, would require criteria to determine which of several acceptable principles were preferable in specific circumstances.

Management and Auditors
The debate was complicated because the responsibility for the contents of financial statements was shared between

management and the independent auditors. It is well established that management has primary responsibility for the
statements through which it discharges its own accountability. Most managers are likely to feel that this responsibility
entitles them to select those accounting principles which they
believe are most appropriate for their own companies.

The auditors, however, have a separate and distinct responsibility, involving significant legal liability, to report
whether or not, in their professional opinion, the financial
statements are fairly presented in accordance with generally
accepted accounting principles.

If unnecessary obstacles to comparability were to be
removed, it seemed clearly necessary for the auditors to point
out any deviation from preferred practices not justified by
differences in actual circumstances. Consequently, it was
decided that auditors should disclose any departures from
pronouncements of the Accounting Principles Board. It
would then be up to the SEC, the stock exchanges, investment advisers, and investors themselves to determine whether
the statements were acceptable or not.

The board issued pronouncements indicating preferred
principles in many important areas, including accounting for
leases, pensions, nonoperating gains and losses, income taxes,
convertible securities, and intangible assets—all areas in which
wide diversity of practice had previously existed—as well as
in many other areas where refinement of financial reporting
seemed desirable.

From time to time studies were conducted to determine
whether changes should be made in the board's structure and
procedures. As a result many improvements were made. But
criticism continued. It was charged that progress was too slow;
that corporate managements had too little voice in the board's
decisions or, on the other hand, that they had too much influence; that the board's pronouncements were too detailed
and too technical; and that differences of opinion within the
board resulted in compromises which weakened its final
conclusions.

The Financial Accounting Standards Board

In 1971 the AICPA appointed a prestigious Study Group
on Establishment of Accounting Principles, headed by Francis

M. Wheat, a former member of the Securities and Exchange Commission and a practicing lawyer. The group included three certified public accountants, an accounting professor, the financial vice president of a large corporation, and a financial analyst. The group was asked to review all criticisms and suggestions and report its recommendations.

This Wheat Commission, as it came to be known, received many written briefs and memoranda. It also held an open hearing, at which oral testimony was recorded. It studied all available writings bearing on the problem before it. Its final report, submitted early in 1972, recommended fundamental changes in the process of establishing financial accounting standards, as follows:

1   Creation of an independent Financial Accounting Foundation, governed by nine trustees representing auditors, financial executives, financial analysts, and accounting professors.

2   Appointment by this foundation of a Financial Accounting Standards Board composed of seven *full-time*, *salaried members* with no other affiliations, supported by an able technical staff.

3   Appointment by the foundation of a Financial Accounting Standards Advisory Council, representing various interested groups, to work closely with the Standards Board in an advisory capacity.

This report met with immediate endorsement by all the organizations concerned, financial support was assured, and in March 1973, the Financial Accounting Standards Board was established.

Implicit in the new approach of the FASB is recognition that financial accounting standards should be in the public domain, that there is a vital public interest in their development, and that experts supported by private organizations sharing responsibility for results can probably do a better job than a governmental agency.

The FASB has issued several Statements of Financial Accounting Standards and many Interpretations; several exposure drafts of possible standards are under consideration; and many additional projects are actively under study. The

standards that have been issued deal with such matters as
foreign currency translation; reporting gains and losses from
extinguishment of debt; accounting for research and development costs, for contingencies and for marketable securities.
Currently being considered are such accounting issues as: a
conceptual framework for accounting and reporting; price
level adjustments; reporting for segments of a business enterprise; criteria for determining materiality; and accounting for
business combinations, pensions, and leases.

The history of the efforts to improve corporate financial reporting over a period of nearly fifty years vividly dem-
onstrates the economic, social, and political importance that
accounting has attained in the eyes of the public.

Summary

Because of the role accounting plays in measuring the
results of business activity and its relationship to the several
functional areas of business (finance, production, marketing,
and economics), accounting has a pervasive influence upon
society. There are few individuals who are not directly or in-
directly involved with some type of accounting report—the
product of the accounting process.

Accounting reports are designed to serve the needs of
various users, such as managements, regulatory agencies,
shareholders, creditors, and the general public. External financial reports are based on "generally accepted accounting
principles." The development of accounting principles has
been a slow evolutionary and controversial process. This is
not surprising, since this process has involved a variety of conflicting interests and since there is no scientific basis for prov-
ing that a given principle is either right or wrong. Honest
opinions differ as to which method of treating a particular
type of transaction will be most useful to those who use financial statements as information for making decisions.

Substantial progress has been and is being made—the
result of the combined and cooperative efforts by several professional groups, such as the FASB, CASB, AICPA, AAA,
NAA, FEI, and SEC. Financial reports today are much better
than they were twenty-five years ago. It can be claimed that

investors and credit grantors in the United States are provided with more useful financial information than those in any other country in the world.

Discussion Questions

1   What is accounting's role in the operating cycle? Explain how the role of accounting is unique when compared with the functions of finance, marketing, economics, and production.

2   What is the primary influence on accounting practice?

3   What influence does the SEC exert on the establishment of accounting principles?

4   What factors necessitated the discontinuance of the APB and the subsequent establishment of the FASB?

4
Financial Reporting

The basic financial statements are the balance sheet, the income statement, and the statement of changes in financial position.

At first glance they seem quite simple and precise. However, for a company of any size, they are not. These comparatively brief summaries of the results of countless transactions require the accumulation, classification, analysis, and interpretation of masses of underlying data. These processes require not only technical knowledge and skill but also experience and objective judgment of the highest quality.

Still, one may reasonably ask why financial accounting has to be so complicated. Most individuals know what they own and what they owe and can calculate their incomes for a month or a year by comparing their bank deposits and withdrawals. Why is it so difficult for a business to furnish statements providing the same sort of information? This was answered in part in the previous chapter by considering the activities of business itself, which must be reflected in the financial statements. The following brief discussion is intended to provide a general impression of the nature of these basic statements. The reader should not be concerned if it does not answer all questions that come to mind. For further information, consult one of the many excellent textbooks that discuss the subject thoroughly.

The Balance Sheet
The balance sheet has long been regarded as of prime importance. It purports to show the financial position of an

Balance Sheet at December 31, 19- -

Assets
Current Assets

Cash	$ 5,000	
Accounts receivable	15,000	
Inventories	30,000	
Prepaid expenses	1,000	**$51,000**
Property, Plant, and Equipment		
Land	$ 2,000	
Buildings	15,000	
Machinery and equipment	28,000	**45,000**
		$96,000

enterprise at a given point in time, usually the end of an accounting period, which is customarily one year, either a calendar or fiscal year.

The basic structure of a balance sheet is shown above. (The captions are self-explanatory, except perhaps for "Inventories," which, in a manufacturing operation, stands for raw materials, work in progress, and finished goods.)

This example of a balance sheet is extremely oversimplified. Additional items, parenthetical explanations, and references to footnotes would normally appear. Other titles and captions may be found in some corporate reports and textbooks. However, the example is adequate to illustrate the basic format.

It should be noted that owners' equity—the amount representing the owners' share of the assets—is the difference between total assets and total liabilities. In arithmetical form, Assets – Liabilities = Owners' Equity, or as transposed on the balance sheet, Assets = Liabilities + Owners' Equity. (This is why the totals on both sides are exactly equal, which confuses some of the uninitiated.) It follows that owners' equity is not represented entirely by *cash*, but by an *amount*, to which a dollar sign has been affixed, representing the difference between dollar amounts ascribed to *all* the assets and *all* the liabilities. In other words, the owners' equity usually resides partly in land, buildings, and machinery and partly in accounts receivable and inventories as well as in cash.

Balance Sheet at December 31, 19- - (cont'd)
Liabilities and Owners' Equity
Current Liabilities

Accounts payable	$ 4,000	
Loans from banks	20,000	
Accrued taxes	2,000	**$26,000**
Long-Term Debt		13,000
Owner's Equity		
Common stock	$23,000	
Retained earnings	34,000	57,000
		$96,000

How precise, then, are the dollar amounts ascribed to
these items? Cash in banks is usually accurate enough (unless
banks should fail). Accounts receivable (uncollected bills),
however, are subject to some erosion through failure of some
customers to pay their debts. Normally, an allowance for bad
debts is deducted from the total of uncollected amounts to
provide for this unhappy probability. But the amount can be
based only on past experience and a guess about the impact
of existing economic conditions. The point is that an element
of judgment about future events, an estimate, is inherent in
this dollar amount, which seems so precise.

How about inventories—raw materials, work in progress,
and finished goods on hand? They are stated at the lower
amount, either what they cost or what they may be sold for.
The dollar amount ascribed to them is inevitably based on an
assumption that they will be sold at some price. Unforeseen
events—sudden style changes, a new invention by a compet-
itor, an economic depression—could wreck that assumption.
Again, judgment about future events must enter into the
accounting.

Land, buildings, and machinery are stated at cost (what
was paid for them). But buildings and machinery wear out
with use or may become obsolete even before wearing out; it
cannot be assumed that they will continue to be worth what
they cost. So an amount is deducted each year to reflect the
exhaustion of a portion of the cost through use or the mere

passage of time. This deduction is called a charge for depreciation and is usually based on estimates of the useful life of the building or machine, again involving judgments about the future.

Enough has been said to indicate the nature of the difficulties encountered in presenting the financial position of any continuing enterprise at any given time. These and other complex questions must be dealt with in preparing balance sheets of large corporations.

At one time, the balance sheet was considered the basic statement. For one thing, bankers who lent money to a company were keenly interested in how and when it would be repaid. They wanted to know about the current assets such as cash, accounts receivable, and inventories, which are usually quickly convertible into cash and on which they could "pounce" if the borrower failed to pay up. This is still true to some extent.

It was assumed that stockholders could tell how the company was doing by comparing one year's balance sheet with the next. If owners' equity increased, even after dividends had been paid to stockholders, all would seem to be well. But as the numbers of stockholders proliferated and they became more remote from management, they needed more information about the operations of the company: how the profits were made; how the increments to owners' equity were generated. Fewer and fewer stockholders regarded themselves as permanent owners of shares in the company. They could sell their shares on the open market; they could buy more or simply hold what they had. The decision (involving allocation of the stockholders' resources) depended largely on the company's prospects, its "earning capacity." And the best available basis for judging the future was information about its operations in the past: Were operating profits increasing? Investors as well as creditors needed this information to judge the risk of loss.

The Income Statement

As a result, the focus of interest shifted to the income statement (also called the profit-and-loss statement), which

Income Statement for Year Ended December 31, 19--

Revenue

Sales	$100,000	
Other income	1,000	**$101,000**

Costs and Expenses

Cost of goods sold	$70,000	
Depreciation	2,000	
Selling and administrative expenses	13,000	
Interest	2,000	87,000

Income before Taxes	**$14,000**
Provision for Income Taxes	6,000
Net Income for the Year	**$ 8,000**

previously had been a highly condensed and relatively uninformative document. The income statement, now considered essential, discloses the results of operations for a business for a period of time.

A greatly oversimplified example of an income statement is shown above.

Again, a real corporation's income statement would usually be more extensive than this. The arrangement and the captions would often be different. Footnotes would explain unusual items.

An important recent change is to show on the income statement the net income per share of common stock. This is obviously of vital interest to individual stockholders. If net income is $8,000 and there are 8,000 shares of stock outstanding, only one dollar of net income is attributable to each share. But since net income, like owners' equity, is rarely represented by an equivalent amount of cash, the probability is that "dividends" paid out to stockholders would not exceed fifty cents a share. Each stockholder can decide whether this return, in light of what he paid for stock, its current market value, and the company's prospects, is sufficient to justify holding the shares.

The dividend is an amount determined by the board of directors to be distributed to stockholders as a return on the investment they have made in the company. Adequate dividends, paid regularly, naturally help to make the stock an attractive purchase, and this enables the company to raise additional "risk capital," if desired, more readily than otherwise.

The net income per share is commonly described as *earnings per share* and often symbolized in financial analyses as EPS.

The amount of net income not distributed as dividends is retained for use in the business and is designated as an addition to *retained earnings*, shown on the balance sheet as a part of owners' equity.

Most corporate income statements also show the changes in retained earnings following the net-income and earnings-per-share figures. Sometimes a separate statement of changes in retained earnings is presented. First, the balance of retained earnings at the beginning of the year is shown, then net income for the period is added (or net loss is subtracted), then dividends paid are subtracted, and finally the balance of retained earnings at the end of the year is shown.

It is difficult to grasp the significance of the net income figure and of the earnings-per-share figure without understanding the nature of the items in the income statement.

Revenue from sales represents not only actual payments for goods or services sold during the period but also deliveries resulting in claims against purchasers who may pay their bills later (represented by accounts receivable on the balance sheet).

"Other income" is usually interest on investments and miscellaneous items not related to operations.

The cost of goods sold (consisting of material, labor, and other costs directly related to production of the goods) is often deducted from the sales figure before presenting other income and expenses.

Depreciation is a charge against revenue to reflect the exhaustion of service of a portion of the cost of buildings and machinery. As noted earlier, the same charge is deducted from the original cost in stating the amount at which these assets are carried in the balance sheet. It will be recalled that depreciation is based on an estimate of the future useful life of the assets, so it cannot be presumed to be precisely accurate.

Sometimes depreciation is included in cost of goods sold, since it is directly related to the production of goods. When it is a significant amount, however, many companies prefer to state it separately.

Selling and administrative expenses are the costs of marketing and general management.

The figure for income taxes may also prove to be less than precise, since adjustments may have to be made after the Internal Revenue Service has examined the company's tax return.

It is the accountant's job to see that all estimates are as realistic as possible in the light of the best information available. The basic objective is *to match revenues with expenses*, "input" from operations with "outgo" attributable to the same operations.

To illustrate, a corner drug store has sales of $400,000 for the year. The owner had to pay $275,000 to suppliers for the amount of inventory (drugs, cosmetics, ice cream, etc.) that was sold in generating the $400,000 sales. The owner also had to pay employees' salaries, store rent, utilities, insurance, and some other miscellaneous expenses totaling $85,000. After properly matching the revenues (sales) for the year with the expenses (costs) incurred to generate the revenue, the owner, in this illustration, has earned a before-tax profit of $40,000.

Cash Versus Accrual

Generally, the results of operations for corporations are reported on an accrual basis rather than on a cash basis. Accrual accounting records and reports the *effects* of transactions *in the time periods to which they relate* rather than reporting when cash is received or paid out. Cash receipts and payments are often not valid criteria by which to report operating results. Payments received in advance for magazine subscriptions, to be earned upon publication in the following year, for example, would not be included in revenue for the current year but would be reflected on the balance sheet as a liability. Nor would cash paid out for a new machine be included in current expenses. This would distort net income for the period.

On the other hand, depreciation does not represent a cash outlay of the current period, as already explained, but an allocation of a portion of a cost incurred earlier, which is properly attributable to operations of the current year.

Most individuals and some nonprofit organizations can provide satisfactory reports on a cash basis. Normally, their cash receipts and disbursements will reflect with reasonable accuracy their actual transactions, since accounts receivable, inventories, and depreciation, for example, are not likely to be significant. If there are slight distortions, they are not likely to be too high a price to pay for greater simplicity in the accounting process.

But it would clearly be misleading if business organizations presented investors and lenders only with a statement of cash received and cash disbursed within a given time period. It would be impossible to tell the extent to which the owners' equity was increasing or decreasing. For example, if merchandise is sold at a profit, but paid for on a contract, the owners' equity is increased even though the cash has not

---

Statement of Changes in Financial Position
for Year Ended December 31, 19--

Source of Working Capital

Net income for the year	$ 8,000
Depreciation (not requiring use of working capital)	2,000
Issuance of common stock on conversion of long-term debt	1,000
Proceeds from sale of machinery and equipment	1,000
	$12,000

Disposition of Working Capital

Expenditures for property, plant, and equipment	$ 3,000
Reduction of long-term debt	2,000
Retirement of preferred stock	1,000
Dividends paid	4,000
	$10,000
Net Increase in Working Capital	**$ 2,000**

all been collected. If expenses have been incurred to make these sales, even though they have not yet been paid, the owners' equity is decreased.

This is not to say that the flow of cash is unimportant. It is possible for an enterprise to present a balance sheet showing a substantial owners' equity and an income statement showing a satisfactory profit but still to lack sufficient cash to meet its monthly payroll or to pay interest on its debts or other obligations. This can be the result of the firm's tying up too much money in inventories or in plant and machinery or of the failure of the firm's customers to pay their bills promptly. Usually it is possible to borrow money for short periods in these circumstances, but if the firm has already borrowed up to the limit, it may be in serious trouble. Management of cash is therefore a very important matter, and it is naturally of interest to investors and credit grantors. The need for information concerning cash flows and working capital flows is satisfied by presenting the third major financial statement—the statement of changes in financial position.

Statement of Changes in Financial Position

The statement of changes in financial position supplements the balance sheet and the income statement. It is sometimes referred to as a funds flow statement and reflects the sources of funds (inflows) available to a business and the use of those funds (outflows) during a period of time. An oversimplified example of a funds statement, one emphasizing working capital, is shown on page 48.

Working capital is the excess of current assets (consisting primarily of cash, accounts receivable, and inventories) over current liabilities, or "net current assets." Working capital, basically, represents the resources available to keep the business running from month to month.

It will be noted that the statement shown includes proceeds from issuance of additional common stock and from sale of machinery and equipment, as well as net income from operations. The statement of changes in financial position thus provides a useful link between the balance sheet and the income statement and also between successive balance sheets.

Assumption of Indefinite Life

It is necessary for accountants to assume, unless there is evidence to the contrary, that a business entity will survive indefinitely. The fact that it exists at all shows an intention to make a profit. Unless misfortune overtakes it, neither an accountant nor anyone else can predict a terminal date for its activities.

This inescapable assumption of indefinite life (also known as the "going concern" assumption) affects the reporting of results of operations for short periods, such as one year. The matching of costs that are expected to benefit a number of future periods with the related revenues of successive periods is an exercise in judgment, not an application of mathematical formulas.

It can be said, therefore, that apportionment of the results of transactions that occur in one time period to reported results of operations in other time periods is based on the *probability* that the business will continue, that its assets will be usefully employed, that most of its customers will pay their bills, that the banks in which its cash reposes will not fail, and so on.

Thus accounting must deal with uncertainties as well as with historical facts, and this is one reason why a high level of professional judgment is required of accountants. Yet financial reports are presented in terms of dollars, which appear to be definite and precise. This can lead to misunderstanding on the part of people unfamiliar with the subject. However, no acceptable substitute for measuring diverse business transactions has been developed.

Costs Versus Value

Present accounting principles require that financial statements be based on costs, not on current values, of the assets employed. Not everyone agrees that this principle produces the most useful results. The balance sheet, for example, does not reflect the current value of land, buildings, and machinery, except, perhaps, in parenthetical supplementary information or footnotes.

On the other hand, if it is not the intention to sell these assets, it is of little use to the stockholder to know what they could be sold for. And if they are to be employed in continuing operations, it is assumed that the difference between what they cost and the revenues they produce will constitute the profit or loss that signifies success or failure. This reasoning, in turn, is based on another assumption, that the monetary unit, the dollar, is stable—that it is really a common denominator.

Stability of Monetary Unit

It is clear that the purchasing power of money does not remain the same. Inflation has depreciated the currencies of most countries, including that of the United States. Inevitably the question arises whether the traditional basis of financial accounting—"the cost principle"—continues to be useful in these circumstances.

For example, if a company built a plant in 1960 at a cost of $1 million, with an estimated useful life of twenty years, and used a straight-line depreciation method, it could properly charge off $50,000 a year as depreciation. But if inflation persisted, it could be argued that by 1980 it would require much more than aggregate depreciation charges of $1 million to recover the real purchasing power originally invested. In each of the intervening twenty years, according to this reasoning, profits would be overstated (and taxed unfairly) because the depreciation charges did not reflect the erosion of the purchasing power of the $1 million initial investment.

In some countries the authorities have permitted adjustment of costs based on economic indexes to reflect current purchasing power, so financial statements would not conceal the erosion of capital by inflation. Many American accountants have argued for similar accounting procedures, and authoritative professional societies have recommended supplementary statements in addition to the traditional statements, which would adjust the figures to the "price-level" basis.

However, there is opposition to a complete transition to price-level accounting and abandonment of the customary statements, partly because of disagreement as to the reliability of economic indexes available and partly because of fear that the public would have difficulty in interpreting state-

ments showing not actual dollar results but results in terms
of dollars adjusted by economic indexes—a new common
denominator.

Special Reports

As indicated in the previous chapter, other statements
are required to satisfy the needs of special types of organizations, special situations, or the special needs of intended users.
There may be a need for greater detail in some cases as well
as supplementary schedules of various kinds.

While the underlying concepts are much the same, different recipients have different requirements. The banker,
the investor, the governmental regulatory agency, the tax collector, the manager, for example, all want information for
different purposes, and the nature and extent of the information for each purpose will vary accordingly.

Nonetheless, essentially the same elements are involved
in nearly all financial reports: assets, liabilities, owners' equity,
revenues, costs, expenses, and net income or loss.

It should be noted that not only the stockholders, creditors, or other interested outsiders but also the top management of any organization—the chief executives and the board
of directors—need reports on the financial position and operating results of the *organization as a whole*. These reports to
management are not essentially different from those sent to
stockholders, although usually they are prepared more frequently and in much greater detail.

Summary

This chapter has focused on the three major types of financial statements published by large corporations—the balance sheet, the income statement, and the statement of
changes in financial position. In the aggregate, these corporations are owned by tens of millions of stockholders, including pension funds, trust funds, mutual funds, and insurance
companies as well as other organizations and individuals. It
is on these primary financial statements that public interest
and political concern are concentrated. It is toward their im-

provement that most accounting research has been directed, and it is with them that most professional controversy has been concerned.

Only a few of the major problems encountered in financial reporting have been discussed. There are countless other problems, and even those briefly outlined here need analysis in much greater depth.

The immediate purpose, however, is not only to indicate that financial reporting is not simple, that it cannot transform uncertainties that are a part of economic life into certainties, but also that financial reporting is essential, dynamic, constantly changing, constantly improving in the crucible of criticism and controversy.

Accounting is a discipline based on a body of knowledge that includes concepts, theories, principles, procedures, and techniques. As in other disciplines, this body of knowledge has evolved over a long period of time, but in recent decades the evolutionary process has been accelerated. Basic assumptions are being challenged, refinements of existing procedures are being advocated, and extensions of the ac counting process into new and unfamiliar areas are being urged.

These first four chapters have attempted to provide a bird's-eye view of what accounting is and how it became what it is. Inevitably, broad generalizations have been employed, and terms have been used in some instances without definition. The next few chapters will provide additional explanation, beginning with a discussion of auditing.

Discussion Questions

1   Define assets and expenses and explain their relationship.

2   What does the owners' equity of a corporation represent?

3   Explain why interest has shifted from the balance sheet to the income statement.

4   Why must judgments and estimates enter into the preparation of accounting reports?

5   Explain why matching revenue with the expense that generated it complicates the accountant's job.

6   What is a primary weakness of a cash basis of accounting?

5
Auditing

Several references to auditing have been made in preceding chapters without explanation of this important accounting function.

Auditing is a process of investigation, inspection, analysis, testing, and checking as a basis for professional opinion. It is often referred to as the "attest function." The word *attest* is used by accountants in the primary sense of "to bear witness to," not in the secondary meaning of certifying as true or correct, which would be inappropriate in an area involving estimates and judgments. Thus auditing deals with evidence and judgments related to the reliability of that evidence. It adds credibility to representations made by others. It is a kind of quality control concerned with the quality of data (its existence and accuracy) from which management information is derived, the quality of the information itself (its validity and relevance) as a basis for managerial decisions, and the quality of external financial reports (their fairness) through which managements discharge their accountability to outsiders and from which external users make credit and investment decisions.

It has been said that without auditing, degeneration of the accounting process sets in. This is true not only because of possible fraud through manipulation of accounting data and possible carelessness or ignorance in the classification of data, but also because in a rapidly changing environment an entire accounting system could become obsolete (inadequate for the changing needs of the business or unnecessarily expensive for what it produces). In these respects, auditing is both a preventing and a correcting factor.

It follows that auditors must be skilled accountants and possess wide knowledge and discriminating judgment. The notion, sometimes found among unsophisticated observers, that auditing consists merely of checking the arithmetical accuracy of numbers provided by someone else, is hopelessly unrealistic.

There are several aspects of the auditing function. Internal auditors, full-time employees of large organizations, inform management; governmental auditors are concerned with the quality of information required by their respective agencies for their several purposes; and independent auditors— public accountants serving clients on a fee basis—express a professional opinion on the quality of information provided by their clients to outside interests, such as investors and credit grantors.

To an extent these various aspects of the auditing function are interrelated. For example, independent auditors may rely on information provided by internal auditors as they satisfy themselves, by testing transactions on a sample basis, that both the underlying information system and the internal audit procedures are sound. On the other hand, a governmental agency making loans to businesses of a certain type may rely on financial reports attested to by independent auditors instead of sending its own auditors into the field.

For a small business that cannot afford an internal audit staff, an independent certified public accountant may see to it that management is provided with the information it needs, may also audit its financial reports for submission to banks, for example, and may prepare its income tax returns. In a large organization these tasks are likely to be divided between internal staff and independent auditors, although usually with consultation between them.

It should be emphasized that auditors at all levels make creative inputs. They are not solely concerned with correcting mistakes or preventing irregularities: They are alert to opportunities for improvement in organizational structure, in operating procedures, and in the decision-making arrangements of management itself.

Evolution of Auditing Standards and Procedures

In the early days of business activity, when organizations were comparatively small, when their capital was provided mainly by a few owners, and when their organizational structures were comparatively simple, audits consisted largely of a detailed check of the bookkeeping records against underlying documents evidencing purchases, sales, receipts, payments, bank balances, materials and goods on hand, contractual commitments, debts, receivables, and other transactions affecting financial position and operating results. The purpose of auditing was widely regarded as prevention or detection of error or fraud.

As organizations grew larger and more complex, safeguards against error and fraud were built into internal structures. Additionally, insurance assumed a larger role in providing protection against potential losses. This had to be. Reliance on periodic audits to ensure reliability of internally generated information would not only be prohibitively costly but would also leave gaps between audit dates during which serious irregularities might occur.

In the natural course of events, procedures were developed by which independent auditors could satisfy themselves as to whether or not internal controls and internal audits justified reliance on the data provided by an organization's information system. These procedures included: (1) testing the system by careful study of the internal controls and by auditing selected transactions; (2) securing independent confirmations (of samples of accounts receivable, for example); (3) physical inspection of selected tangible assets (notably inventories); and, (4) analysis of sales, gross profits, cash flow, taxes, and other transactions among which reasonable relations should exist. In later years, the science of statistics has been employed in the sampling process.[1] If these procedures raised doubts about the reliability of the internally generated data, additional audit steps were undertaken. If not, the inspection process could be kept to the minimum necessary to satisfy the auditor that the data were reliable.

[1] Statistical sampling is now considered an essential element of auditing. For a discussion of its application in auditing see, for example, Henry P. Hill, Joseph L. Roth, and Herbert Arkin, *Sampling in Auditing*, The Ronald Press Company, New York, 1962; *The Accountant's Magazine*, Institute of Chartered Accountants of Scotland (July 1971), 369-377; *Management Accounting*, National Association of Accountants (December 1970), 42-44.

As the focus of public interest in accounting centered on corporate financial reports because of the rapidly increasing millions of stockholders, the scope of the independent auditor's role expanded. Emphasis shifted from prevention or detection of errors or fraud to the "fair presentation" of financial statements in accordance with generally accepted accounting principles and also to "adequate disclosure."

Fair presentation requires reasonable estimates and informed judgments involving, in part, future probabilities. Fair presentation also requires application of appropriate accounting principles in given circumstances. But even if judgments and principles are sound, failure to disclose significant information having a material impact on a company's fortunes might be misleading.

The independent auditor thus came to be regarded as a kind of monitor (attestor) of management reporting. The auditor was expected to prevent not only erroneous information, but also excessive optimism or conservatism and any distortion of the information provided through bias or omission.

However, as has been pointed out, it is well established that the primary responsibility for financial statements rests with the management of the organization concerned. The independent auditor's responsibility is to conduct an objective examination of management's accounting, within the framework of authoritative standards. Because no such standards had been developed, difficult questions arose as to what the auditor's responsibility was when there was disagreement with a management decision for which there was nevertheless a respectable precedent. It was also unclear, and still is to some extent, what the responsibility of auditors is for failure to discover errors or irregularities or even unsound judgment on the part of the management. There was need for a reliable statement of the independent auditor's duties.

The Federal Reserve Board became involved in the problem because of its interest in and relationship with banks making loans in partial reliance on audited financial statements. In 1917 after consultation with the accounting profession, the Federal Reserve Board published a bulletin outlining the steps that should be taken in a typical audit of a medium-sized manufacturing or merchandizing concern. This helped establish authoritative auditing procedures.

In 1929 this bulletin was revised to emphasize the auditor's right to rely on an adequate system of internal control and on the use of tests, when internal controls were reliable, instead of on detailed verification of numerous transactions. It was also stated, for the first time officially, that testing and sampling would not necessarily disclose all frauds or other irregularities concealed by the manipulation of accounts.

Similar statements were recorded as part of the documentation supporting the agreements with the New York Stock Exchange, published in 1934. In addition, the primary responsibility of management for accounting judgments was affirmed. Also, pointed reference was made to the concept of "materiality." This concept recognizes that items that do not significantly affect the overall financial position or net income—that is, which are not material in amount—need not be disclosed in financial statements. The concept is similar to the legal maxim, "The law does not concern itself with trifles."

Of major importance was the development of a new, standard form for the independent auditor's report, which was more informative than those previously in use. It described the nature of the auditor's examination and established the language in which the auditor expressed his professional opinion that the financial statements "fairly present, in accordance with accepted principles of accounting consistently maintained by the Company during the year under review, its position at December 31, 1933, and the results of its operations for the year." With some modifications this standard form of representation by independent auditors has prevailed in its essentials to the present day.

Of course, it was clearly understood that if an auditor could not give unqualified approval to the financial statements within the constraints indicated, the exceptions, reservations, qualifications, or supplementary explanations should be noted.

All these developments helped to clarify the responsibility of auditors. But many related questions remained unanswered. Some of them were raised in lawsuits or in cases investigated by the SEC. In an effort to answer them, the national organization of certified public accountants began in 1939 to issue a series of Statements on Auditing Procedure, which outlined recommended steps to be taken by independent auditors in various circumstances. This process continues to the present time. In addition, a statement of Generally Accepted Auditing Standards was developed with official approval, which broadened the conceptual basis of the auditor's responsibility.

Some gray areas remained, however. It was subsequently decided that auditors should not express opinions on financial statements if certain exceptions or qualifications were so material or if restrictions on the scope of the auditors' examinations were so significant as to raise doubts as to the validity of the financial statements taken as a whole. Later, it was also decided that in such cases auditors should state clearly that they were not in a position to express opinions on the financial statements taken as a whole and should indicate their reasons. Further, "adverse opinions" were required in cases where auditors believed the statements to be *not* fairly presented. In short, everything possible was done to minimize misunderstanding as to the responsibility assumed by an auditor in various situations.

Disclosure

One area of financial reporting that has been hard to define is "disclosure." How much detail should be presented? How much supplementary explanation is necessary? What unusual transactions or situations should be highlighted? These are questions not susceptible to precise and comprehensive answers. Yet independent auditors constantly have to answer them.

Management is usually reluctant to make disclosures that might be helpful to competitors. Prior to the creation of the SEC, for example, many companies did not report revenue from sales in their income statements. They feared such disclosure would hurt their competitive position. This information is clearly useful to investors, but it was difficult for auditors to insist on its disclosure by one client when competitors were not obliged to follow suit.

However, much progress has been made. Statements showing current position and operating results in comparison with those of the preceding year are standard. Many companies publish ten-year summaries of earnings. Earnings per share are now covered by the auditor's opinion, as part of the formal financial statements. Formerly they were reported separately and were calculated by a variety of formulas. Disclosure of sales and profit information by major segments of diversified companies (product-line reporting) is now required. Large gains or losses from transactions not related to regular operations must now be set forth separately in the income statement as "special items." "Contingent liabilities." such as claims in pending lawsuits or disputed tax assessments, must be disclosed in the financial statements.

Footnotes explaining the significant accounting policies followed and other items in the financial statements are found in most corporate annual reports. Indeed, some stockholders complain they are confused by getting too much information. However, professional investment advisors, who have become more and more influential, can utilize this information and continually ask for more.

The accounting profession has initiated many of the disclosures that have become customary, only a few of which have been mentioned here as examples. The SEC, of course, has required many others. Statements filed with the SEC, which are available although not readily accessible to the general public, contain more detail than those ordinarily sent to stockholders, many of whom prefer short summaries showing overall results.

It is probably impossible to foresee all possible situations that should be disclosed in order to make financial statements "not misleading." Hindsight often shows that it would have been wise to disclose information that did not seem vitally important at the time. But the trend has been toward more disclosures, and it seems certain to continue under the unrelenting pressures of the SEC, the financial analysts, the accounting profession itself, and last but not least, the courts.

Legal Liability

Officers and directors of corporations are subject to serious legal liabilities for improper conduct, and so are independent auditors like all professional practitioners.

Lawsuits involving claims of many millions of dollars have been filed against managements and accounting firms on the basis that the financial statements for which they had a share of responsibility contained misleading information or failed to disclose information whose omission made the statements misleading.

Rarely have accountants been charged with deliberate intent to deceive. Rather, it is usually alleged in such cases that negligence is involved, that is, the accountants have performed their work without due care: for example, by failing to discover irregularities, by failing to point out the inadequacy of provisions for bad debts, or by failing to disclose the composition of collateral pledged to secure a loan.

In other words, accountants acting as independent auditors can be sued for alleged failure to exercise sound professional judgment: for example, judgment in selecting audit samples or in taking additional audit steps when tests show doubtful results, judgment in estimating the probability that customers will pay their bills, or judgment in deciding whether an unusual situation should be disclosed or not.

The general legal principle underlying accountants' liability is that anyone offering a specialized service to the public who does not have the degree of skill commonly possessed by others in the same work commits a species of fraud on those who employ him.

There is a presumption that accountants should not be held to a standard higher than that recognized in their profession. Accordingly, official pronouncements by professional accounting societies or authoritative studies indicating what is considered good practice—which are admissible as evidence in a court—serve as a protection against unreasonable claims against accountants who comply with such statements.

On the other hand, those who depart from them may be called upon to justify their position in court. To the extent, therefore, that authoritative standards can be established and published by the profession, by the SEC, or by both, the resolution of difficult questions by the painful process of litigation may be avoided. However, in a few cases auditors have been charged with criminal conspiracy to defraud. If a jury finds the defendants had "guilty knowledge" of important information that was not disclosed—and the judge accepts that finding—the fact that usual auditing procedures were followed may not be a sufficient defense.

Strengthening the Auditor's Position
The pressures of public expectations, reflected in court decisions and SEC regulations, continue to expand the scope of the independent auditor's responsibility. This topic is of such current import that the American Institute of Certified Public Accountants has appointed a special seven-member study commission to consider what should be expected of independent auditors. At the same time, the auditor's importance and influence have been greatly strengthened. For one thing, as a general rule, the SEC and the New York Stock Exchange will not accept financial statements if the auditor's "opinion" (report) contains any exception or qualification. This means if an independent auditor disagrees with management about the accounting treatment of a material item, the difference must be reconciled before the required financial statements can be filed with the supervisory authorities.

Furthermore, the SEC requires explanation of the reasons for changing independent auditors. This is intended to discourage managements from discharging auditors because of disagreements on matters of principle.

There is also a trend toward creating corporate audit committees, composed of members of the boards of directors who are not full-time officers of the companies and to whom the independent auditors have direct access at all times. Such committees can enlist the power of the full boards in resolving any differences between the auditors and the executives of the companies.

All in all, the visibility and the prestige of independent auditors have increased enormously over the past fifty years. Yet pressure for expansion of their scope continues. The dynamism characteristic of the accounting field as a whole is clearly evident in the audit function. Research in this area has been intensified, and exciting possibilities for the future are being widely discussed in both academic and practitioner circles.

Impact of the Computer

There are tens of thousands of computers being utilized in businesses throughout the United States. The introduction of these computers into management information systems is having a significant impact on auditing. Formerly, data were recorded on paper and were supported by business documents, both of which left a so-called audit trail which could be checked. Data are now stored on magnetic tapes, invisible to the human eye. Furthermore, transactions can be created and destroyed by computer programs, creating an increased opportunity for manipulation and/or potential fraud.[2] Auditors have had to learn to satisfy themselves as to the validity of data by analytical methods and by tests run through the computer itself. The result has been to minimize the detailed checking of the traditional documentary evidence and to increase utilization of techniques designed to check on the controls and programs of the computerized accounting systems. The expected result is a decline in the number of auditors engaged in the examination of documents and a growing demand for auditors with higher levels of technical skill and analytical ability.

The computer also processes data at high speed and low cost (after the initial investment), which opens the door to retrieval of quantities and varieties of information that it would be prohibitively expensive to develop by manual methods. As will be shown in a later chapter, access to this vastly

---

[2] Recent cases involving computer fraud or embezzlement include the $1 million Los Angeles Telephone Company equipment theft, the $1.5 million New York Union Dime Bank embezzlement, and the $300 million Equity Funding Insurance Fraud. See Jack F. Thorn, "Control of Computer Abuses," *Journal of Accountancy* (Oct. 1974), 40, and Don B. Parker and Susan Nucum, "The New Criminal," *Datamation* (Jan. 1974), 57.

expanded source of information is invaluable to management in its planning, control, and decision-making processes. But the availability of additional information also whets the appetite of investment analysts and credit grantors for more disclosures in financial reports, for which independent auditors may be called upon to assume their appropriate share of responsibility.

Extension of the Attest Function

Most of the preceding discussion has focused on the audit of published financial statements of corporations whose securities are widely distributed to the public—corporations subject to the requirements of the SEC and the stock exchanges. This is naturally the area of greatest public and political interest. But auditing occurs in ever more widening fields.

Millions of smaller businesses and nonprofit organizations also need independently audited financial reports for bank credit purposes or for regulatory agencies of the government or for the protection of their directors or trustees. Implicit in any activity involving the use of other people's money is accountability for results in the form of financial reports; and if such reports are not audited, they are becoming less acceptable.

As mentioned earlier, the independent auditor's act of reporting his professional opinion on the fairness of financial statements has come to be known as the attest function. This function is gradually expanding to include opinions on information other than balance sheets, income statements, and statements of changes in financial position. For example, there is current debate on the appropriateness and feasibility of auditing, or at least "reviewing," the interim quarterly reports of corporations. The Small Business Administration asks independent auditors to attest to compliance of Small Business Investment Companies with regulations not directly related to financial transactions. Hospital costs reimbursable by the federal government under Medicare may be attested to by independent auditors. Housing authorities have required independent audits of construction costs of housing projects financed by governmental agencies.

These, however, may be only straws in the wind. It has been widely suggested that professional accountants attest to forecasts, primarily projections of future operating results—not, of course, as factual representations, but as estimates soundly conceived and based on reasonable assumptions. Possible attestation of income tax returns has been discussed, as well as cost data used in negotiating government contracts and in fixing rates to be charged by public utilities.

Professional accountants may properly attest to the reliability of systems of internal control under certain conditions. Imaginative accountants have suggested that in due time they may attest to the adequacy of management information systems as a whole for internal purposes. Even an audit of overall "management performance," according to standards yet to be developed, has been the subject of serious professional discussion.

More recently, proposals have been offered for development of reporting standards for costs involved in antipollution measures taken by companies to protect the environment, to which auditors may be asked to attest.

It is becoming increasingly apparent that auditors may attest to any representations related to management information if there is sufficient reliable, objective evidence on which they are competent to base their professional opinion and if standards are developed to govern the nature and scope of their investigation and analysis. The form of the attestation would differ, naturally, according to the type of information involved. For example, the standard form of auditor's report on the customary financial statements would be inappropriate in attesting that forecasts were soundly conceived and based on reasonable assumptions.

Current speculation about such possibilities suggests that public demand will result in extensions of the accountant's attest function, not only in familiar financial areas but in heretofore unexplored fields.

Summary
Auditing is an indispensable adjunct of accounting. It helps prevent deterioration of the underlying data on which

accounting information is based. It adds credibility to the information in the hands of those who rely on it in forming decisions.

The independent audit, resulting in attestation by professional accountants, has evolved from a somewhat restricted service to one of vital public concern. In the early days such audits were intended to provide reasonable assurance that financial statements were in accordance with the books and to prevent or discover fraud. Now they are designed to provide reasonable assurance that the statements are fairly presented in accordance with a growing and increasingly rigorous body of standards.

Thus the responsibilities of independent auditors to the investing public, to creditors, and to clients have increased enormously.

Heavy legal liabilities have been imposed on auditors, the limitations of which are not yet clear. Until they are clarified, auditors may hesitate to extend their attest function into unfamiliar areas.

Yet there is perceptible public interest in such extension and enough speculation in professional circles to suggest that gradually it will come about.

In the traditional area of financial reporting the independent audit serves not only as an element of protection to investors, creditors, and others who use the information but also as protection to management, directors, and trustees against charges that they have not taken all reasonable precautions to ensure the reliability of their representations.

Thus auditors serve both client and public, including government, in the communication of information essential to the continued health of the economy.

Discussion Questions

1 Describe the nature of auditing.
2 Describe the unique role played by an auditor in the business community.
3 In what way is auditing preventive in nature?

4   How do you perceive the task of the internal versus the independent auditor?

5   Is it fair to hold auditors legally liable, considering the small percentage of a company's accounting system they examine? If so, when?

6   Explain how the computer has simplified the auditor's job, while paradoxically making it more complex.

7   What are some of the areas being mentioned as possibilities for extension of the attest function?

6
Managerial Accounting

Managerial accounting is sometimes referred to as though it were entirely separate from financial accounting, which has been the primary emphasis of the preceding chapters. Actually, they both belong in the category of accounting as described in Chapter 1.

It is true that accounting as a discipline or organized body of knowledge developed most rapidly in response to pressures for useful financial reports. Very early, British laws required corporations to submit independently audited financial statements to stockholders, and much later, similar requirements were imposed by the Securities and Exchange Commission in the United States.

As a result, independent auditors were the first accountants to feel the need to secure professional status (see Chapter 8) and to develop standards justifying public confidence. They had the strongest influence on the development of accounting theory and principles, which in turn influenced the design of management information systems. So, for many years, the dominant concern of accountants was with the financial accounting of corporations.

This situation changed rapidly after World War II. As the number and size of corporations rapidly expanded, managerial accounting for decision making, planning, and control moved toward the center of the stage. An extensive literature was produced, research was sponsored, and accounting education was expanded in new directions. The advent of the computer and the emergence of mathematical aids to decision making added new and fascinating dimensions to the structure of managerial accounting.

It needs to be emphasized, however, that so-called financial accounting and managerial accounting are simply different facets of the same thing. They are not mutually exclusive. The data for both come from the same sources. Both are financial, and both are managerial. Clearly, management plans, controls, and decisions are ultimately directed toward achieving desired financial results—the effective allocation of resources in terms of money. On the other hand, corporate managements are also vitally interested in maintaining access to credit and capital markets through acceptable financial reporting. So it can be said that financial reporting is also an essential part of managerial accounting.

To be sure, the basic data are arranged in different ways, presented in greater or less detail, and have a more or less comprehensive scope, since they are prepared for different purposes. But both financial reporting and managerial accounting are necessary parts of the broad accounting discipline.

Decision Making

Management decisions are required concerning both continuing activities of an organization and proposed new activities. In either case the decision may concern broad policy or a specific, isolated problem.

Every organization must choose among alternative goals it would like to reach. A manufacturing business, for example, may choose to produce one or a few items for sale, or it may choose a whole range of related or diverse items. The alternative courses of action are many. To make a decision without adequate information would be foolhardy.

Suppose that the addition of a new product is under consideration. The following questions must then be considered: Are adequate supplies of the necessary raw materials available, and at what cost? What investment in new machinery and in labor would be required? What sales of the new product could reasonably be expected, and at what price? What is the nature of competition? What selling expenses would be involved for advertising, direct-mail solicitation, sales representatives' calls, and delivery of the product to the customers? If sales are made on credit, what are probable losses from failure of customers to pay their bills?

As these initial questions are answered, more are raised: What volume of production, in the light of answers to the previous questions, would probably yield a reasonable margin of profit? Up to a point, the cost of each unit of product becomes less as the numbers of units produced increase. Yet the production of more units than could be sold at a satisfactory price could result in serious loss.

The launching of a new product involves initial expenditures that cannot reasonably be expected to be recovered from sales immediately. How many years will it probably take to recover the initial costs and begin to derive a profit from the new product? Could the money to be devoted to launching and continuing production of the proposed new item be put to better use? If interest rates are high, any free funds in the organization might be invested in bonds more profitably than in the new product. All possible consequences of the new venture must be evaluated.

Equally important decisions affect the existing operations of an enterprise. Examples are reflected in questions like the following:

Are all the products equally profitable? Should any be dropped in order to concentrate effort on those that are more profitable?

Is too much money tied up in supplies of raw materials and the accumulation of unsold finished products (inventories)?

Would it be more economical to buy parts to fit into the product from an outside source or to make the parts within the organization?

Is it better to pay premiums for fire insurance or to set aside funds to cover possible losses or simply to accept the risk involved?

Is the cost of serving customers outside a readily accessible area so great as to make it unprofitable?

Are prices adequate to cover rising costs due to inflation? If they are not, will competitive conditions permit price increases? If they will not, how can costs be reduced?

If additional capital is needed to finance rapid growth in the volume of business, should the money be borrowed from banks or should bonds or additional shares of stock be issued?

The questions go on, almost endlessly. The answer to each question is a decision, even if it is a decision to do nothing. In each case information is needed, and the process of accumulating relevant, valid data and converting them into information is an accounting function. These oversimplified sketches of business problems are used merely to indicate the nature and variety of data needed for sound decision making.

The data come from the organization's own information system, which yields records of past experience from engineers' estimates, from surveys of consumer needs and attitudes, from industry statistics furnished by trade associations or government agencies, from expert knowledge of company officers and employees, and from many other sources.

Accountants must classify and analyze, test for validity and relevance, and convert the raw data into information that is useful for the management team with whom the responsibility for decision making lies. Not all the data are factual. Estimates and probabilities are also important. The recent growth in the use of mathematical decision theory is the result of efforts to identify and improve the degree of reliability that can be placed in them.

Traditionally, accounting has not been a decision-making profession. Recently, however, accountants have become important members of the management team and are now expected to be able to analyze, interpret, and communicate the data they collect in light of a company's competitive environment and operations, thus contributing to effective decision making. More and more corporate chief executives have accounting backgrounds.

Planning

If a decision is reached to embark on a course of action, a plan for its implementation is necessary. The plan should include: (1) the delegation of responsibility for executing various parts of the venture, such as financing, purchasing, production, sales, collections; (2) a synchronized timetable setting target dates for completion of each step in the process; and, (3) a *budget* for estimating expenditures and revenues expected.

The budget is an accounting tool. In addition to being a part of the plan, it becomes a control instrument. By comparing actual results with the budget, management can tell whether the plan is going as expected. Accounting also provides the feedback enabling management to continually evaluate the results of the decision. The budget can be modified in the light of actual results, or the decision can be revoked—the whole project can be called off to minimize losses if it seems doomed to failure.

Budgeting

A budget is simply an estimate, a projection, of what is expected to happen in the future, based on experience, all relevant information, and the best judgments available. Since what actually happens will not coincide precisely with the forecasts, budgets are most useful if they are adjusted to conform with reality as often as practicable—quarterly, monthly, or even weekly, if that close a watch over operations is desired and seems worth the cost.

A simple statement comparing the budget of a small organization with actual results might be as shown below on page 76.

The deviations from the estimates shown in the statement may not be alarming. Seasonal or other factors could explain the differences. But with this information, management knows in which areas to seek explanations. For example, in the Sample Corporation illustration, management would seek to learn why sales decreased, whether cost of goods sold decreased proportionately to sales, and especially why selling expenses increased even though sales decreased. In real life these items would usually be broken down into component parts: sales, into different products or different territories; cost of goods sold, into labor, materials, and other direct costs; selling expenses, into advertising, sales representatives' expenses, and delivery costs; administration, into salaries and expenses of the major management groups (production, marketing, finance, and so forth). The objective is to bring deviations from the plan to light soon enough to do something about them, if necessary, and to identify the executive responsible for the part of the operation affected.

Sample Corporation

Income Statement Budget Comparison

	Actual 19--	Estimate 19--	Difference 19--
Revenues			
Sales	$100,000	$110,000	($10,000)
Other income	1,000	2,000	(1,000)
Total revenues	$101,000	$112,000	($11,000)
Expenses			
Cost of goods sold	$ 70,000	$ 75,000	($5,000)
Depreciation	2,000	2,000	-0-
Selling expenses	11,000	10,000	1,000
Administration	5,000	5,000	-0-
Interest	2,000	2,000	-0-
Taxes	6,000	7,000	(1,000)
Total expenses	$ 96,000	$101,000	($5,000)
Profit	$ 5,000	$ 11,000	($6,000)

In organizations of any size the overall operating budget would be based on departmental budgets, or "cost center" budgets. These would include in greater detail the estimates of actual costs of each part of the operation. Periodic reports from each center would enable management to trace the source of significant variations from the budget.

In a complex manufacturing operation making a variety of products, budgeting naturally is a complex process. Managements should know the contributions to profit or loss of each product, and budgets should indicate how many units of each product must be sold, at what price, to produce desired results. This requires sophisticated analysis, especially in deciding how much of the unavoidable cost of maintaining the plant, regardless of whether anything is produced or not, should be absorbed by each product.

In addition to operating budgets, well-managed companies usually prepare cash budgets and capital expenditure budgets. Cash budgets show amounts of money needed month by month. These amounts will vary according to the timing of tax and interest payments, for example, and the sources and amounts of cash available to meet the requirements. Capital expenditure budgets show, for example, plans for additions to, or replacement of, plant and equipment or for acquisition of other companies and the financial resources required.

Budgeting is a useful, indeed an indispensable, tool for any organization and for individuals and families as well. There are many different approaches and techniques involved. Budgets must be tailor-made to fit the particular needs of specific organizations, but general principles and procedures have been developed that accountants can apply to almost any situation.

In government and in some other nonprofit organizations, the budgeted "revenues" are in fact "appropriations," that is, authorizations to spend the amounts indicated for the purposes set forth in the expense items. Theoretically, this puts a limit on the amounts to be spent. Since there is no direct relation between expenditures and revenues in most nonprofit activities, a limitation of this kind seems desirable. Thus the term *budget appropriation* has become a familiar phase in government parlance.

However, the rigidity thus introduced into budgeting of this type can have some strange consequences. If the administrator spends more than the amount appropriated for one purpose but less for others, authorities are usually inclined to let the differences "wash out." But if he overspends the total amount appropriated, nothing much can be done about it except to fire him or approve a "supplemental appropriation." The latter is a frequent solution.

Conversely, if the administrator approaching the end of the year finds that significantly less than the total appropriation has been spent, the temptation is to search for ways to spend more—usefully or not—for fear the authorities will reduce the appropriation for the following year to the amount of this year's actual expenditures. This temptation is not always resisted, and the results can be extremely wasteful.

Effective budgeting in any situation requires reliable cost accounting, which in itself is a specialized area but one which is inextricably linked with both financial reporting and management planning, control, and decision making.

Cost Accounting

Almost all management decisions require consideration of costs. Erroneous estimates of costs can wreck a product or a company: If cost estimates are too high, a product or service may be priced out of a competitive market; if they are too low, pricing may produce a loss instead of a profit. Inadequate analysis of costs can defeat cost control. Waste and inefficiency can increase costs unnecessarily. Both cost estimating and cost control require valid data reflecting the separate elements of cost. The cost of manufacturing a product includes the distinct elements of raw materials, labor, use of plant and machinery, and *overhead* (administration, insurance, electricity, and other costs essential to the operation).

Materials, labor, and any other costs that rise or fall as production is increased or decreased, such as the cost of parts purchased from outside, are known as *variable costs*. Plant and machinery and overhead—to the extent that their costs do not vary with production—are regarded as *fixed costs*. The sum of fixed costs and variable costs is the real cost of the product. Or is it? How good are the data?

The allocation of overhead is one of the most difficult problems of cost accounting. Should part of the president's salary be charged against each specific product? Probably not; the president would be there whether that product were produced or not. How about the salary of the person in charge of the workers directly involved in the production of a product? Probably. Then what about salaries of all the people between the president and the direct supervisor? And how much of the cost of telephone bills and travel, electricity, rent or depreciation of buildings, insurance premiums, and so on, should be allocated to each specific product? In the end, these decisions must be arbitrary, but they will be most successful if made in the light of full information and clear recognition of the consequences of all possible alternatives.

In the time period between the purchase of raw materials and the receipt of revenue from the sale of finished products, a substantial amount of money is tied up in the manufacturing process. If the money is borrowed, interest must be paid; if the company uses its own cash, interest must be sacrificed. Interest is also an element of cost.

Costs do not cease when the finished product emerges from the factory. It must then be sold and delivered to customers. Advertising and direct selling expenses and shipping and warehousing costs must be taken into consideration when prices are determined.

But prices cannot be fixed to cover costs plus a profit without regard to the market. It is what customers are willing to pay that governs price, and this in turn depends largely on the extent of competition.

The unit cost of standardized products normally goes down as the number of units produced goes up. This is partly because of the spreading of the fixed costs over the larger number of units, partly because of economies in purchasing raw materials in large quantities, and partly because of utilization of labor and machinery with maximum efficiency, that is, with the least possible idle time.

Consequently, manufacturers strive to increase sales volume. They may set prices below cost in order to capture a larger share of the market, in the expectation that when volume reaches a certain point, unit costs will have decreased far enough that the same price will yield a satisfactory overall profit.

A refinement of cost accounting that increases its usefulness is known as *standard costs*. It consists of developing standards, based on experience, for both fixed and variable costs, against which actual costs in each category can be compared. "Variances" between actual costs and the standards come prominently to management's attention, and appropriate action can be taken, which can sometimes mean the difference between profit and loss.

The expense of developing and administering a standard cost system may not be justified by its benefits in a small organization with limited volume of sales, but standard costs have proved their value in larger and more complex organizations. The accountant must be able to recognize when such a system would be advantageous and recommend its use to other members of the management team.

Direct costing is another refinement that has proved useful in many situations. Under this system only variable costs directly related to production are charged to product costs.

Fixed costs, such as depreciation of buildings, taxes on land, and overhead, are written off against income in the time periods to which they relate. This is not generally regarded as acceptable for external financial reporting purposes, but it can aid management decisions. For example, in a slack time it may show that it would be better to continue production, even if only direct costs could be recovered, than to lay off employees and leave a plant idle, since fixed costs cannot be avoided in any event.

Decisions to sell at prices below full cost may be made for other reasons. If an information system readily yields data on which estimates can be based both on a direct and full-cost basis, management is likely to make the most intelligent decisions.

Control

The relation of accounting to control has been mentioned in connection with budgeting and cost accounting, which, in addition to being parts of the planning process, also permit comparison of actual results with the targets that have been established. But accounting is concerned with other kinds of control as well.

Internal control is essentially an arrangement of organizational structure—a division of duties and work flow among employees—designed to minimize the possibility of error or fraud and to assure the accuracy of records insofar as possible. Accountants have pioneered in the development and refinement of internal control systems because as auditors they rely to a large extent on such systems.

Inventory control is a common accounting problem. The objective is to assure a steady flow of raw materials to the production process without tying up too much cash in excessive supplies, and to assure an adequate supply of finished goods to meet customers' demands without having to store unneeded quantities of unsold products. Frequently, the needs will vary from season to season. A system that yields information on when to order materials, how much to order, and when to slow down or speed up production is the control device.

Cost control is an ever-present concern. Cost-accounting systems are designed and administered by accountants, and special cost studies are often conducted. Since every phase of a business involves costs—financing, purchasing, production, marketing (yes, and even accounting!)—a continuous flow of information is essential to prevent waste, inefficiency, and unnecessary expenditures.

These are only a few examples of the uses of accounting information in the control function.

While manufacturing companies may have the most complicated problems to resolve, similar processes of decision making, planning, and control are required in agricultural, mining, and service industries, and in nonprofit organizations. The questions in each case may be different, but the underlying objective is the same—allocation of resources to best advantage. Nor does the size of the organizational unit alter this basic objective. The largest and smallest corporations, the government, the university, the golf club—all have to decide, plan, and control if they are to attain their objectives. Of course, not all of them do.

These functions can be carried out well or badly. The top manager of any organization may rely on personal knowledge and intuition instead of acquiring adequate information. And it may work, or it may not. Information may be developed by people who are not trained accountants. It may be adequate, or it may not.

However, as the techniques of data processing and of accounting become more refined, and as competition in a complex society becomes more keen, it stands to reason that the organization which takes advantage of accounting knowledge and integrates the accountants' skills with those of other management personnel will have the best chance of success.

Operations Research

The application of scientific problem-solving approaches to managerial problems is described as *operations research* or *management science*. Mathematical and statistical tools are employed in efforts to predict the probable effects of alternative courses of action. Computers greatly facilitate this process.

For example, in considering the launching of a new product or the expansion of facilities to increase output of an existing product, "models" can be constructed showing probable results based on a variety of assumptions about costs, sales, volume, and price. On the other hand, a system can be made more effective by means of operations research; for example, a system of inventory control. Operations research can help to determine when to order more materials and how much to order.

Mathematical approaches can also help to answer questions like the following: Should products be shipped by water, rail, truck, or plane? Should warehouses be established at certain strategic geographical points? What will be the probable incidence of style changes? What should the staffing of restaurant tables be at different hours of different days? How many trucks are needed by a fuel oil distributor? How many sales representatives should be hired and where should they work?

To get the same results in large-scale enterprises by using pencil, paper, and arithmetic would be prohibitively expensive. Only the mathematical short cuts and the computer capacity for rapid processing of masses of data make operations research a practical business tool.

Of course, it is on the accuracy of the data used as input that the validity of the solutions depends. Some of these data must be estimates, but most will be financial and operating data supplied by accountants. The integrity of the data is critical if the accountant's contribution is to be effective. Also, some factors cannot be quantified—human behavior, like the reactions of employees or customers, for example. Yet, though perfection may be unattainable, the analytical approach, complemented by management's experience, judgment, and even intuition, is likely to lead to better decisions than subjective judgment and intuition alone.

Operations research, largely concerned with costs of alternative actions, is so closely related to accounting (some claim it is a part of accounting) that accountants should have at least a general understanding of its uses and methods. Many public accounting firms offer operations research as part of their professional services.

Behavioral Science

The art of management has been defined as getting things done through other people. Organizations are composed of people. Human motivations and human reactions to environmental changes have been the subject of increasing research in management circles in recent years.

Accounting, with its influence on the allocation of resources and on managerial planning, control, and decision making, has a significant impact on people.

A budget, for example, sets targets of performance and limits of expenditures for a group of people. If it is imposed from above, it may be resented and resisted. If it originates with the group itself, it may be padded with protective devices. Only through consultation, participation, and mutual understanding can best results be obtained. The accountant is often the mediator in an effort to build a workable budget.

Control measures like time-and-motion studies (or even audits) may reduce employee morale and incentive if introduced in a manner that suggests distrust on the part of management.

Innocent cost allocation patterns may spark wasteful internal conflicts if division managers feel they are being charged with a disproportionate share of overhead. Supervisors have shown reluctance to confer with the boss if their departments are charged for his time.

Incentive bonuses may tempt division managers to pull sales into the current period and push expenses into the next period, thus distorting the financial statements.

Financial reports to investors and bankers may influence them in the allocation of resources at their disposal. If the reports do not communicate effectively, if they are subject to misinterpretation, they may arouse resentment against the issuer.

All this simply suggests that accountants should be aware of the needs and probable reactions of the people who will use, or will be affected by, the products of their labors. Many an accountant has been disappointed at the failure of a system or designed procedure, which, despite its technical soundness, was misunderstood by, or was unacceptable to, the people on whom its implementation depended.

A basic understanding of psychology and sociology, with emphasis on the study of behavior of formal organizations, and fundamental training in communication theory are recommended parts of an accountant's education.

Information Systems

Most of the data on which planning, control, and decision making must be based come from an organization's "information system," and so do the data required for external financial reporting. The importance of an adequate information system, therefore, cannot be overestimated.

Every organization has an information system, good or bad. In a proprietorship the system may reside in the owner's memory or on the backs of envelopes in the lining of a hat or in a checkbook. In a small to medium-sized organization the double-entry bookkeeping system is likely to be the only information system. In a large, sophisticated organization a centralized information system, mechanized or lodged in a computer, will provide most of the data needed for all purposes by all personnel concerned with planning, control, and decision making in any phase of the organization's activities. All sorts of intermediate arrangements are possible between the extremes.

The design and installation of information systems is an accounting function, whether executed by trained accountants or not. A basic bookkeeping system is almost always the first formal information system. It is a response to the essential need for data required for tax returns, for financial reports to banks or other credit grantors, and for management's appraisal of the financial results of the total enterprise activity.

But in an organization of any size or complexity this is inadequate for several reasons. First the ordinary bookkeeping system is designed to yield aggregate data, readily assembled in summary form in balance sheets, income statements, and income tax returns. Second, the accounting principles governing inputs to the system are only those acceptable for financial reporting and tax purposes.

Such a system will not provide sufficient details of the

costs of producing, advertising, selling, and delivering manufactured goods, for example. Or the information it does provide may result in erroneous decisions. For example, it is acceptable for financial reporting and tax purposes to assume that the raw materials most recently purchased are the first to be used in the manufacturing process. In a period of rising prices the most recently purchased materials are the most costly. The result is lower reported profits and income taxes than if the cost of the first materials acquired were included in the cost of goods sold. But in deciding whether or not to raise the price of a given product, it might be wiser to assume that its real cost is based on the average cost of all the raw materials on hand.

For tax purposes it is also possible to charge against revenues higher amounts for depreciation of plant and machinery in the early years of their use and correspondingly declining amounts in the later years. But for cost accounting purposes this practice might be unsatisfactory.

In the absence of a centralized information system yielding the data they need, the managers of the several segments of a business—production, marketing, personnel, etc.—are likely to develop their own information as best they can, to make their own plans, and to justify their own contributions to the total effort. But what they develop will be based on different assumptions and will not tie in with the "official" bookkeeping system. The effort to supply their own information will distract them from their primary duties. And top management may have trouble in deciding which information is "right."

Clearly, the design of an information system should meet the specific needs of an individual organization. It must be tailor-made. The capacity of management personnel to understand and use it properly must be appraised. The cost of installing and operating the system in relation to probable benefits must be considered. And the system should be flexible enough to permit its expansion as the organization grows, without taking it apart and starting over. Systems design presents accountants with stimulating challenges to their ingenuity, as the system must be able to generate the kind of data needed in the decision-making process.

Summary

The elements of capital investment, revenues, costs, and expenses enter into both management decision making and external financial reporting. But the basic data constituting these elements are like building blocks that can be arranged in different configurations for different purposes.

A financial report to stockholders may, quite properly, differ in some respects from a financial report of the same entity to the Internal Revenue Service (income tax return). The objectives and guidelines are different. And the determination of costs for purposes of a management decision may be different from determination of similar costs for either financial reporting or tax purposes. Again, the objectives and guidelines are different. The accountant, as a member of the management team, can understand these differences and therefore contribute significantly to the success of a company's operations.

It follows that no single objective or set of guidelines should dominate the information system. Ideally, it should yield all relevant data for the objectives of the organization, subject to the constraint that expected benefits must justify their cost.

Discussion Questions

1   Why are accountants qualified to be a part of the management team involved in decision making?

2   Explain the relationship between managerial and cost accounting.

3   Costs are often classified as fixed or variable. Explain the difference between fixed and variable costs.

4   What is the significance of a budget?

5   What are standard costs? How do they relate to budgets?

6   How is the budget of a nonprofit organization different from that of a profit-seeking firm?

7   What is the relationship of behavioral science to managerial accounting?

8   How does operations research impact on accounting?

7

Income Tax Accounting

Regardless of occupation or type of business, almost all individuals and businesses are required to pay income taxes. These taxes are computed by multiplying applicable rates times taxable income. Income tax rates are set by law by various governmental units. Determining the amount of taxable income to which the rates are applied is a highly specialized field. Income tax accounting is a form of financial reporting as well as a critically important ingredient of managerial decision making. This chapter presents an overview of this highly technical and important subject.

Nature of Taxable Income

As has been explained earlier, an important function of accounting is to periodically measure the results of operations for a reporting entity. The income statement shows this information. It is based on generally accepted accounting principles whose objective is to provide guidelines for proper reporting.

An income tax return is essentially an income statement, but it is governed by special rules, some of which differ widely from generally accepted accounting principles. Yet, the data on which a corporation's tax return is based are derived for the most part from the financial information system that also yields the data for the income statement sent to stockholders. The *process* of preparing the return is also an accounting process, but the concepts, methods, principles, and rules are in many respects different for income tax purposes. Taxable income, therefore, may not reflect what actually happened, but what the government decides is the amount to be taxed.

The distinction between taxable income based on internal revenue regulations and "book income" based on generally accepted accounting principles is important. The purpose of levying an income tax is to raise revenues for governmental units. The underlying laws and regulations are therefore directed toward assessment and collection of those revenues. The purpose of determining book income is to provide various individuals with an objective and reliable measure of the actual results of operations of the reporting entity. The underlying accounting principles are therefore directed toward realization of earned revenues, whether or not collected, and the proper matching of expenses. Given different purposes, one should not expect taxable income and book income to be identical.

Special Provisions
A few of many possible examples will illustrate some of the differences between taxable income and book income. One method of determining the cost of materials flowing into the production process out of inventories is to assume that the materials most recently purchased are the first to be used. (Accountants call this the last-in, first-out method, abbreviated LIFO.) In a period of rising prices, this means the most costly materials are the first to be used, thus increasing the cost of goods sold and decreasing net income, in contrast to the results of assuming that the materials first purchased were the first used (FIFO), or averaging the cost of all materials in inventory to calculate the cost of goods sold.

The last-in, first-out method is regarded by some accountants as appropriate when the materials are all alike; for example, bushels of wheat in a grain elevator, where the last bushel poured in is considered the first to come out. The same reasoning can be applied to tons of ore, gallons of oil, and similar materials.

However, when the tax law permitted the LIFO method to be used, many different types of industries adopted it in order to reduce current taxable income. This occurred even though many accountants felt LIFO was inappropriate for some industries, both for financial reporting and management decision purposes, as it tended to understate net income by charging a higher inventory cost than other inventory methods which were in general use.

On the other hand, tax laws sometimes result in what accountants consider overstatements of income by distorting the matching of costs against revenues of a given year. For example, cash received as payment in advance for services to be rendered in a following year has been held to be revenue in the year of receipt for tax purposes. Also, the estimated costs of rendering future services on products sold during a given year have not been allowed for tax purposes in the year of sale but only when the services are actually rendered.

Depreciation of plant, machinery, and equipment is another area of difference. For tax purposes, higher amounts of depreciation may be charged off in the earlier years of use ("accelerated depreciation"). This, of course, results in lower taxable income in those years and higher taxable income in later years, in a sense deferring a portion of tax liability for a time. But in financial reporting to stockholders many companies taking advantage of accelerated depreciation for tax purposes prefer to spread depreciation charges evenly over the years of the useful life of the assets. In such cases, rather complex accounting adjustments are necessary in order to prevent investors from overlooking the deferred tax liability, which may reduce income in the later years of the useful life of such assets. Equally troublesome is a special investment tax credit that Congress on different occasions has enacted into law in order to encourage businesses to purchase new plants, machinery, or equipment. The objective has been to stimulate the economy and increase employment. Two ways of accounting for this credit have been held acceptable: Either reduce income tax payable in the year the asset is purchased, thus increasing net income substantially in many cases in that one year, or spread the tax saving derived from the special credit over the useful life of the asset purchased. Most corporations prefer the first method because of the immediate tax benefit. Many accountants complain that this can result in increasing reported profits materially in one year by spending money for new assets, thus distorting the trend of earnings per share. This question has been the subject of vigorous controversy.

A problem of a related nature arises in the so-called natural resource industries—those removing irreplaceable assets from the earth, notably oil and gas but also coal and certain other materials. The cost of these raw materials, naturally, must be charged against revenues as the materials are used. The cost is allocated according to the quantities removed. The charge is known as *depletion* and is similar to depreciation of fixed assets. The total cost is incurred at one time. In subsequent years, appropriate portions of the cost are charged against revenues produced by the use of the asset. However, special provisions of the tax law permit certain affected industries to take a specified tax deduction for depletion in every year in which the natural resource produces income. This "percentage-depletion" allowance is based on the gross income so produced and is not related to the cost of the natural resource. In contrast to depreciation of other assets, the total of the annual percentage-depletion tax deductions can be greater than the original cost of the natural resources. This percentage-depletion concept is not acceptable for financial reporting purposes, but it can, of course, increase profits by reducing taxes.

There are other ways in which income tax accounting differs from generally accepted accounting principles, but these examples will suffice for present purposes.

Influence on Financial Accounting

The income tax has inevitably influenced accounting practices—not always for the better, in the opinion of some accountants. Neither business executives nor individuals enjoy paying taxes. Business executives are naturally inclined to adopt accounting methods resulting in the lowest immediate tax. Accountants who audit financial statements issued to investors and creditors prefer accounting methods that fairly present financial position and net income in accordance with generally accepted accounting principles. In some cases, however, such principles have been modified to accommodate tax considerations.

The LIFO method of costing inventories, described earlier, is permissible for tax purposes only if it is also used for financial accounting and reporting purposes, according to a

Treasury Department rule. Even though some accountants dislike the use of this method by certain industries, the profession has felt obliged to recognize it as generally accepted.

In the case of accelerated depreciation, however, accountants have declared that generally accepted principles require disclosure and adjustments when this method is used for tax purposes and another method is used for financial reporting.

Both indicated ways of accounting for the special investment tax credit to purchasers of new plant, machinery, and equipment have become permissible by law and therefore generally accepted for financial reporting purposes, much as many accountants dislike the use of the full credit to increase net income materially in a single year.

On the other hand, percentage depletion, permitted for tax purposes, is not acceptable for financial reporting, as already noted.

If the government should recognize price-level accounting (see Chapter 4) or direct costing (see Chapter 6) for income tax purposes, there would probably be immediate pressures for general acceptance of these methods also for financial reporting.

There is, and doubtless will continue to be, a tension arising from the conflicting motivations of the tax collector, the taxpayers, and the independent auditors.

Tax Planning

In planning and making decisions, managements must be aware of the tax effects of transactions of many kinds. The form or timing of a transaction may result in a higher or lower tax, even though the substance, from an economic viewpoint, would be unchanged if another form or another time were adopted. In some instances, where the government permits alternative accounting methods, the choice of one method over another may result in minimizing tax liability or at least deferring it. Errors, even honest errors, in conforming with income tax requirements may result in heavy financial penalties, in addition to any unpaid tax that may be due. For all these reasons tax planning is an important management function.

It follows that professional accountants, whether they are employed by business organizations or are engaged in public accounting practice, must be generally familiar with income tax accounting. At the same time, unless they specialize in this highly complex field, they should be cautious in deciding or advising how to handle any transaction giving rise to substantial tax liability. A mistake sometimes made is to assume that tax questions may be adequately resolved by the application of general accounting concepts.

How Did It Get This Way?

The general application of an income tax in the United States followed adoption of the Sixteenth Amendment in 1913, which provided that "The Congress shall have power to lay and collect taxes on incomes, from whatever source derived, without apportionment among the several States, and without regard to any census or enumeration."

Congress applied the tax to both individuals and corporations. While both are important, the corporate tax is of greater concern to most professional accountants and is the subject to which this discussion is confined.

The initial tax rate on corporation income was 1 percent. Over the years this rate has been increased significantly, to a high of 52 percent. At present, corporations are required to pay the federal government 20 percent on the first $25,000 of taxable income, 42 percent on the next $25,000, and 48 percent of taxable income in excess of $50,000. It should also be noted that in some circumstances taxable income could be greater than net income determined under generally accepted accounting principles.

The Internal Revenue Code enacted by Congress provided, essentially, that taxable income should be determined according to the methods of accounting regularly employed by the taxpayer, *unless* in the opinion of the Commissioner of Internal Revenue such methods did not clearly reflect net income. This, in effect, gave the Commissioner of Internal Revenue power to make accounting rules for tax purposes, subject to legislative instructions by the Congress and interpretation of such legislation by the courts.

Tax Controversies

The determination of corporate net income for a single year involves estimate, judgment, and consideration of future probabilities under *any* set of accounting principles. Amounts to be charged against revenue for depreciation, consumption of inventory of raw materials, and uncollectible accounts receivable, for example, may vary according to assumptions based on experience, prediction, or alternative acceptable rules.

It is clear that the area for difference of opinion between taxpayer and tax collector is very wide indeed. Their objectives, and therefore their assumptions, are different. The duty of the Internal Revenue Service is to "protect the revenue," which essentially means to collect all taxes legally owed without unreasonable delay. The objective of corporate managements, the taxpayer in this case, is usually to pay the least possible tax at any given time without violating the law. Wherever the law is not perfectly clear, the door to controversy is open.

"Avoidance" of income tax by taking advantage of provisions in the law or regulations is perfectly legal. "Evasion" of tax by falsifying or illegally concealing significant information or by willfully failing to file income tax returns may result in charges of criminal fraud with most serious consequences. Most taxpayers try to avoid as much tax as possible without stepping over the line into evasion. Accountants who advise them must be keenly conscious of this distinction. Any legal method of deferring payment of a tax until later, even if it cannot be avoided ultimately, is advantageous, since it releases cash that can be used to augment income during the interim period.

Invitations to controversy arise not only from the inherent difficulties in determining net income for a year but also from obscurities or ambiguities in the law itself or in Internal Revenue regulations interpreting the law. Over the approximately seventy-five years of income tax administration, almost every conceivable type of corporate transaction has been the subject of efforts to put into writing precisely how a transaction should be accounted for in determining taxable income. Since the writing is done by human beings, precision is not always attained, and possible variations in the assumed circumstances are sometimes overlooked. So there are differences of opinion in the interpretation of the rules.

Arguments about the rules take place first at the level of the Internal Revenue Service—the tax collector. After exhausting the appellate procedures within the Service itself, a taxpayer may appeal to the courts. By choosing to go to the United States Tax Court (a special tribunal set up to handle the great volume of tax cases), the taxpayer can defer payment of any additional tax demanded by the Service until the Tax Court has ruled. Alternatively, a taxpayer can pay the tax under protest and sue for refund in a district court. From that court's decision, appeals to higher federal courts may be taken.

The matter is further complicated because different courts, and sometimes even different officials of the Internal Revenue Service, reach different conclusions in similar cases. If the stakes are high, this may encourage taxpayers to gamble on a favorable ruling in a new jurisdiction, even if an unfavorable precedent exists elsewhere. However, litigation is costly, and unless fairly large amounts of money are involved, the matter is usually settled with the Internal Revenue Service.

Enough has been said to indicate why the collection of income taxes has been described by some observers as an "adversary proceeding." It should not be, of course. Payment of taxes should be regarded as a civic duty. The tax law should be simple and equitable. The reasons why simplicity and equity have been elusive will be discussed shortly.

It is easy to see why accountants as well as lawyers have become deeply involved in income taxation. Many have specialized exclusively in this field. It has a fascination for those who like research, meticulous argument, and face-to-face encounters with Internal Revenue representatives. About one-third of the fees of accountants engaged in public practice are believed to be derived from income tax work. Furthermore, an accountant acting as independent auditor must know enough about the subject to judge whether a client's provision for income tax liability is reasonable or not.

Legal Aspects

Lawyers are widely involved in income taxation because there are many legal questions in addition to accounting questions affecting the determination of the tax. And only lawyers are permitted to represent taxpayers in the courts.

In past years some accountants specializing in taxation inadvertently stepped over the line separating accounting from law. There were complaints that they were illegally practicing law without a license. Conferences of representatives of the two professions resulted in a "statement of principles" indicating the proper scope of each but recognizing that in tax matters accounting and law are closely interrelated and that some overlapping is inevitable.

Both lawyers and certified public accountants are authorized by law to represent clients before the Internal Revenue Service. Cooperation between members of the two professions in tax cases involving significant amounts is a common practice. Accountants who are not also members of the bar (as some thousands are) must be careful to avoid incursion into the field of law, which could be damaging to their employers or clients as well as to themselves. Attorneys must likewise be careful not to extend their activities into the realm of accounting, which is beyond their legal and professional qualifications.

Simplicity and Equity

The untidiness apparent in the structure and administration of the income tax law has brought forth many demands for tax reform. Periodically Congress responds to rising public pressure and holds extensive hearings. After all points of view have been aired, amendments to the tax law are drafted. These amendments are designed to reduce the complexity and inequities by closing loopholes presumed to favor the rich and by eliminating special provisions that increase the difficulty of determining taxable income. This draft is then attacked on all sides by groups that would lose some benefit to which they have become accustomed and also by other groups that in the name of equity contend similar benefits should be available to them.

Since members of Congress must be responsive to the

demands of substantial numbers of their constituents and of individual constituents who are unusually influential, the result often is that the effort to produce a greater degree of simplicity and equity in the tax law ends up by adding to its complexity and inequity.

LIFO inventories, which were originally devised for industries using homogeneous materials, have been allowed all industries, even department stores, in the name of equity.

Percentage depletion, originally allowed as a result of persuasive arguments by the oil industry, was later extended to producers of slate and gravel on the same grounds.

Deductions for contributions to educational, religious, charitable, and health and welfare institutions have been attacked, but the attacks are beaten off by powerful reactions of these influential institutions.

Interest on bonds issued by state and municipal governments and their subdivisions and agencies is exempt from federal income tax. Suggestions that these exemptions be eliminated are naturally resisted by the local governments, on the basis that it would force them to pay higher interest rates in order to sell their bonds.

The federal government itself is partly responsible for the complexities and inequities of the tax law. By changing the tax rules to stimulate the economy or to encourage behavior it regards as socially desirable, it adds to the inherent difficulty of pinning down that elusive figure stated as corporate net income for a single year.

It has been suggested from time to time that a tax on gross revenue from sales should be substituted for the corporation income tax. This is resisted mainly because a tax on sales would be passed on to consumers. But, in the opinion of many accountants, the income tax is also passed on to consumers—it is a cost of doing business. It is contended that corporations must produce profits after taxes to stay in business. The money to pay income taxes can come only from customers. Prices must be high enough to produce net income sufficient to pay taxes and leave the necessary profit margin.

Discussion of this point and many others concerning taxation has been going on for years and seems likely to continue. Meanwhile, the cost to taxpayers of complying with

the tax law (in addition to paying the tax itself) and the cost
to the government of enforcing it continue to increase.

Summary

It should be clear even from this brief and incomplete
examination of income taxation that it has a significant effect on financial reporting, on management decision making,
and accordingly, on the design of information systems.

Accountants should know enough about the tax law to
be aware of how it relates to what they do and to the advice
they give. But how much is enough? It is a full-time job to
become truly proficient in this field, requiring not only mas-
tery of basic accounting and tax principles but also awareness
of constant changes in the tax laws, the regulations, and the
decisions of the Commissioner and the courts.

At the minimum, every accountant should be familiar
with the fundamental concepts on which the Internal Revenue Code is founded and with the provisions having the broadest and most frequent applications. Unless one specializes in
taxation, one need not master the details involved in the application of these provisions, but one must be aware of their
existence. The necessity of seeking more competent advice
when facing an unfamiliar question should be recognized.

Discussion Questions

1   Why are there differences between taxable income and
    accounting income?

2   How does accelerated depreciation affect the total tax
    paid over the life of an asset?

3   How do income tax laws influence financial accounting?

4   Why does it seem impossible to develop an income tax
    law that is both simple and fair?

5   Explain the difference between tax avoidance and tax
    evasion.

8
Attaining Professional Status

Throughout the preceding chapters references have been made to *accountants, professional accountants*, and the *accounting profession* without defining these terms. Actually, the words accountant and profession are commonly used quite loosely.

There is nothing to prevent bookkeepers from calling themselves accountants. At the same time, a chief executive of a large corporation or a high governmental official or a university professor or the head of an international public accounting firm may also be described as an accountant. It is also true that many vocational groups refer to themselves as "professions" without having a solid claim to this designation.

There are significant advantages in being a member of a recognized profession. The traditional professions—medicine, law, the clergy—have invested the word with great prestige. The public generally has come to respect and trust professional people, and as a result they have been accorded certain valuable privileges. They are permitted to set their own admission standards, within reasonable limits, as well as their own ethical and technical standards. Only accredited members of the profession are permitted to use certain titles or to do certain work affected with a significant public interest.

With these privileges go responsibilities. The professions are expected to require of their members competence, integrity, and a dedication to public service.

Sociologists have studied the professions as a distinct segment of the pluralistic American society, different from business, government, and nonprofit organizations. As a result of these studies, there is general agreement that a true profession is one meeting all the following criteria:

1   It renders essential services to society and recognizes a social obligation.

2   It is governed by a code of ethical conduct, which is enforced by disciplinary machinery.

3   It has formal requirements for admission of new members and an identifying title that only members are permitted to use.

4   Its members have acquired a body of specialized knowledge, through some system of formal education or training.

5   It is recognized by law.

These criteria are stated in different words by different writers, but there is general agreement on the substance.

Evolution of the Accounting Profession

There have been accountants throughout historical times, but until the nineteenth century their role was that of employee, serving government or business or whoever hired them. As a group, they did not meet the five criteria mentioned.

However, beginning with the British corporation law of 1845, to which reference has been made earlier, a new social need was created—the need for independent audits—which led to the development of an accounting *profession.*

In addition to requiring corporate managers to issue financial statements, the English law required an audit of the records by persons who were not involved in the management. The auditors made a separate report, stating whether or not the financial statements presented "a true and correct view" of the state of the company's affairs as shown by the books.

The need for such an independent check was clear. The

opportunity for fraud, error, or undue optimism on the part of management—with grave consequences to investors—was apparent. Without some assurance that the financial representations of management were reliable, investors would hesitate to risk their money by buying a company's stock.

The degree of assurance provided by an independent audit depended, of course, on the competence and objectivity of the auditors. The basic English corporation law of 1845 provided that accountants could be employed to conduct the audit—a natural provision, since familiarity with bookkeeping and financial statements was necessary to perform the task.

At that time in Great Britain there were hundreds of accountants who offered their services to the public, many on a part-time basis because they held other regular jobs simultaneously. They were self-taught, for the most part, and their abilities varied widely. The title *accountant* was not restricted, and anyone who chose to do so could assume it. There was, therefore, no way of identifying those who were sufficiently competent and responsible to conduct the audits of corporations under the new law.

To meet the obvious need, Institutes of Chartered Accountants were organized under statutory authority (royal charters), first in Scotland in 1854 and then in England in 1880. These institutes set standards for the admission of members, including a period of apprenticeship training and the passing of a written examination. Standards of professional conduct also were developed. Only members of these bodies could designate themselves *chartered accountants*. Accounting publications were launched, lectures were given to the apprentices, and a body of knowledge peculiar to accountants began to take visible form.

For the first time in history, accounting, as represented by the chartered accountants, was recognized as having attained the status of a profession. Its numbers grew rapidly.

The Profession in the United States
While these developments were occurring in Great Britain, the United States was gradually shifting from a predominantly agricultural to an industrial economy. Much of the

capital needed to start new industries came from Great Britain, which was then the banker for the western world. British investors sent their chartered accountants to America to check on their money.

Perceiving opportunities here, many Scottish and English chartered accountants remained in the United States and founded accounting firms, some of which have become among the largest and best known in the world. But there were enterprising American accountants, too, and some of them also established firms that have attained international scope and reputation.

With the example of the British chartered accountants before them, and with the cooperation of those who settled here, the American accountants formed associations and set about obtaining professional identification.

The political structure of the United States—a federation of states retaining a measure of autonomy—dictated a different approach from that followed in Great Britain. There, the accreditation of professionals was delegated to societies authorized by law. In the United States the licensing of professionals was left to the state governments.

Accordingly, the accountants of New York sponsored legislation, enacted in 1896, creating the title *certified public accountant*, usually abbreviated CPA, to be conferred upon candidates who met specified requirements. Other states followed this example, until every state had a CPA law. Gradually the requirements stiffened. First the emphasis was on experience in accounting, with the British apprenticeship in view; written examinations were soon required; then, as the universities introduced accounting courses at a professional level, an increasing number of states included a college education as a prerequisite for the CPA certificate.

While all the states ultimately adopted the two and one-half day Uniform CPA Examination, there continued to be significant variations in other requirements governing education, experience, residence, and recognition of CPA certificates of other states.

Unlike Great Britain, there was no national law requiring independent audits of corporations in the United States until 1933. This may have been partly responsible for the relatively slow growth in the number of CPAs in the early years. Fifty years after enactment of the first CPA law in New York, there were only about 30,000 certified public accountants in the entire country. Thereafter, however, the number grew rapidly, passing 150,000 in the mid-1970s. The federal securities acts of the mid-1930s, requiring independent audits of corporations issuing securities in interstate commerce, were no doubt one stimulus to growth, but the increasing complexity of the American economy as a whole and the extension of governmental regulation have vastly increased the demand for professional accounting services.

The certified public accountants gradually developed standards, professional literature, and policies and procedures squarely meeting the five criteria of a true profession stated earlier. Previous chapters have stressed that accounting services are essential in modern society. The ability of accounting to meet the criteria of legal recognition, admission requirements, and the identifying title have just been described. Later in this chapter the development of formal education in accounting, the growth of a body of specialized knowledge, and the standards of professional ethics for accounting will be examined.

Growth of Public Accounting Firms

The independent audit, as noted earlier, must by definition be conducted by persons not associated with management. This function was naturally assumed by public accounting firms, which offer services to the public for a fee. By 1975 there were more than 15,000 public accounting firms in the United States. They ranged in size from one-man practices serving small businesses to international organizations employing thousands of accountants and maintaining offices in most principal cities of the United States and in many foreign countries.

These larger firms developed concurrently with the rapid growth and geographical dispersion of the giant corporations which engaged them as independent auditors. It was necessary to provide adequate manpower accessible to the branches and subsidiaries of corporate clients in order to conduct the independent audits efficiently and economically.

While the unique role of certified public accountants in public practice as independent auditors was the primary reason for their identification as professionally competent and responsible, their activities are by no means confined to this.

When the income tax laws were enacted, there was a sudden and widespread demand for professional accounting assistance, as well as for legal aid. Tax practice continues to be an important part of the work of the CPA.

Furthermore, from the very beginning, some CPA firms, including some which are now among the largest, developed a strong interest in assisting clients with problems related to internal planning, control, and decision making. These types of activities came to be known as management advisory services and are now a growing part of the practice of many, if not most, public accounting firms.

In conducting independent audits year after year, a CPA firm inevitably becomes familiar with the organizational structure of its clients, their operating procedures, and their financial problems. The accounting firm is, therefore, a natural source of advice and assistance when a client faces a problem involving the analysis, classification, and interpretation of data.

The extent to which this advice and assistance is sought from a CPA firm, however, depends in part on the extent of accounting talent available within the client organization. Most sizable organizations in business, government, and nonprofit activities, employ full-time accountants, often CPAs, as controllers or financial vice presidents, who preside over staffs of bookkeepers and accountants and sometimes specialists in taxation, computer technology, operations research, and the like. In these cases, the CPA firm is likely to be called upon for special services only when extraordinary problems arise requiring knowledge or skills not immediately available within the organization.

Smaller organizations, however, are not usually able to afford a permanent staff of professionally qualified accountants. Accordingly, they frequently consult the CPA firms that conduct their audits for assistance with internal problems, including taxes, financing, pricing, cost control, inventory control, and many others. Thus the CPA firm in public practice, in addition to performing independent audits, fills gaps in the accounting capabilities of client organizations.

Professional Accountants

Who, then, are considered to be professional accountants? Certified public accountants are identified as professionals by their title. However, in addition to those practicing as public accountants, thousands of CPAs occupy executive positions in business and government and posts of professorial rank in universities. There are also other well-qualified accountants in responsible executive or academic positions, whose competence is comparable to that of CPAs but who for one reason or another have not acquired the CPA certificate—a primary reason being that various state laws have historically required experience in public accounting. For example, comparable levels of professional accounting competence are found among the officers and staff of an organization and among the partners and staff of the CPA firm serving the organization. To a great extent, the knowledge and skills of the financial executive and the accountant in public practice are interchangeable. Many CPAs have left public accounting to become controllers of corporations, and on occasion financial executives have left corporations to join accounting firms.

Any discussion of accounting at the professional level, as distinguished from the clerical, record-keeping level, must therefore assume a broad definition of the term *professional*. University professors of accounting, whether certified public accountants or not, offer professional credentials in the form of Ph.D. degrees. They teach the future professional accountants. The academic branch of any profession must be regarded as an integral part of that profession. So the term *accountant*, as used in this book, is intended to mean anyone possessing competence in accounting at a professional level, whether engaged in the public practice of accounting or employed in business, government, education, or a nonprofit organization. There is a definite movement toward elimination of the requirement of public accounting experience for the CPA certificate. The requirement is, in effect, a vestigial survival of the old apprenticeship system. In some states accounting experience in business, government, or teaching is already accepted as equivalent. The national association of certified public accountants has recommended that the requirement of public accounting experience be dropped for candidates who have met suggested educational standards, which are described later in this chapter. If this trend continues, all accountants of professional competence will have the opportunity to become certified public accountants regardless of the field in which they choose to work; they will be able to join the same organizations, to exchange information, and to cooperate in research in all areas of accounting.

Meanwhile, the scope and diversity of accounting activity as it has evolved in the United States may be indicated by listing the leading national associations in accounting:

American Accounting Association
    (mainly academic)

American Institute of Certified Public Accountants
    (limited to CPAs; mainly concerned with public accounting)

Federal Government Accountants Association
    (governmental accounting executives and auditors)

Financial Executives Institute
    (limited to officers of larger corporations)

Institute of Internal Auditors
    (mainly staff of larger organizations)

National Association of Accountants
    (open to all accountants; mainly concerned with industrial accounting)

Other organizations have developed programs to recognize professional competence in particular fields of accounting. For example, the National Association of Accountants has established an Institute of Management Accounting to administer a uniform examination and to grant a certificate in management accounting. Successful candidates become *certified managerial accountants*, CMAs. Basic educational requirements may be satisfied by a bachelor's degree from an accredited college or university or by a satisfactory score on either the Graduate Record Examination or the Graduate Management Admissions Test for graduate studies in business. The Institute of Internal Auditors also gives a uniform examination leading to a *certified internal auditor*, CIA, certificate.

It is too early to determine what influence these programs may have on accounting education or on the interest of industrial and governmental accountants in obtaining the CPA certificate, assuming elimination of the public accounting experience requirement for the latter.

Evaluation of Accounting Education

All professions have developed along similar lines. Individuals with appropriate talents and interests, perceiving a need for a service they feel competent to render, offer their assistance to those who appear to need it. The practitioner is self-taught. If the need is real and the service is helpful, demand for more of it attracts additional practitioners to the field. Apprenticeship procedures are established, through which younger aspirants can learn from established practitioners and also by on-the-job training. As a body of knowledge in the field gradually takes form, schools begin to teach it. The only available teachers are practitioners or former practitioners, and they teach from their experience—how to do it.

In time, however, a literature develops. Research is undertaken. General principles are formulated and tested in practice. Concepts and theories of wide application evolve. Full-time teachers take over the educational process. Meanwhile, the total body of knowledge, both conceptual and procedural, increases rapidly. There comes a point at which the schools cannot accommodate it all.

The history of law and medicine has followed this pattern, and so has the history of accounting. But the professions of law and medicine, as the western world knows them, had their origins in ancient Greece and Rome. Accounting as a process, a technique, is probably even older, but its claim to professional status dates from barely a hundred years ago.

One might say that accountants have been catapulted into the ranks of professionals by the Industrial Revolution, the development of the corporation, and the taxing and regulatory procedures of modern industrial democracies.

The change from self-instruction to apprenticeship to formal instruction in procedures to formal instruction in basic concepts and theories has taken place in a comparatively short time. Indeed, it has not yet been completed.

Not until the very end of the nineteenth century was

accounting taught at a recognized, degree-granting university in the United States. By 1907 it was included in the curricula of only about a dozen universities. At present over 600 colleges and universities offer one or more courses in accounting. But the most extensive offerings are in the undergraduate and graduate schools of business administration at the larger universities.

However, until recently, with some notable exceptions, the teaching was largely descriptive of what happened in the world at large: how corporations reported their financial affairs, how public accountants conducted their audits, how managers determined their costs, and so on.

In 1959 authoritative studies of business education were published, which were sharply critical of undergraduate schools of business administration. Accounting courses did not escape criticism. Many of them were described as vocational training that emphasized procedures rather than basic concepts. They were not likely, it was said, to stimulate students' intellectual growth.

These studies led in turn to the most comprehensive reexamination of accounting education ever undertaken. The results were published in 1967, under the title *Horizons for a Profession*, and were a description of the common body of knowledge deemed appropriate for professional accountants.

It was recognized that accounting, like every other field of knowledge, was changing and expanding in response to society's needs. Accounting courses and textbooks describing how things were being done at any given point in time were likely to become obsolete before long. Accordingly, it was concluded that the formal educational process should concentrate on basic concepts, an understanding of general principles, and a knowledge of techniques only sufficient to equip the student to begin a career as an accountant and to adapt to changing needs.

It was also concluded that students of accounting should be exposed to a broader range of subject matter than had been customary. Greater attention to the economic, social, and political environment in which accounting played its part was recommended. Emphasis was placed on communication—the use of written and oral English. Understanding of the characteristics of formal organizations and the principles underlying management and motivation of people were regarded as essential. Mathematics, statistics, and probability theory were strongly recommended because of their relation to auditing and managerial decision making. An understanding of computers was regarded as indispensable for the same reason. A grasp of the management functions—finance, production, marketing, personnel relations—was also considered necessary, as was some acquaintance with business law. A basic grounding in the humanities, the physical and social sciences, and the arts was assumed to be desirable for any professional person. All the foregoing were proposed in addition to the basic core of fundamental knowledge about financial and managerial accounting, auditing, and taxes.

How could all this material be covered in the time available? It was recommended, first, that five years of college study be required of students who desired to become professional accountants. Second, it was recognized that not all the subject matter outlined needed to be studied in great depth. Conceptual understanding rather than procedural skill was emphasized. It was said that the professional accountant should be *literate* in mathematics, for example, but not necessarily *literary*. This is a way of saying the accountant should be able to "read and write" math without being professionally competent as a mathematician.

Finally, it was recognized that much of the how-to-do-it training in procedures would have to be acquired after graduation. Seeing the handwriting on the wall, the professional accounting societies and many accounting firms had already developed staff training programs and continuing education courses for more advanced practitioners. The scope and variety of these programs, which have the merit of being kept up to date, have continually increased.

This expanded university curriculum was, of course, meant for students who intended to become professional accountants. For students who aim at positions as business executives—the majority of students in any school of business—some grounding in accounting is essential, since it is an important managerial function, but greater emphasis naturally needs to be placed on subject matter closely related to the field in which the student intends to specialize, such as marketing or personnel.

A New Introduction to Accounting

In 1971 a study group of accounting educators, after several years of work, published a report recommending a new approach to the introductory accounting course. Entitled *A New Introduction to Accounting*, the report outlines suggested subject matter appropriate for the first year's course in accounting. It is consistent with the conceptual approach recommended in *Horizons for a Profession*, but goes into much greater detail in describing the topics that might appropriately be covered. It allows for maximum flexibility in actual application but presents "bundles of related ideas" in broad subject areas that the group believed should be covered. It was conceded that modification of the outline would probably prove desirable in the light of experience and that full implementation of the recommendations would have to await development of new teaching materials. The recommended content for an introductory course would include discussion of: (1) the nature and function of accounting; (2) accounting and its environment; (3) the valuation and measurement of economic resources; (4) the transaction approach to accounting measurements; (5) the collection, classification, and transformation of accounting data; (6) financial accounting for profit-seeking enterprises; (7) accounting for individuals and nonprofit organizations; and, (8) managerial accounting. In the body of the report each of these topics is discussed at some length, with suggestions as to how it should be treated.

Courses along the lines recommended have been organized and are being offered at some colleges and universities. The study group report has stimulated changes in textbooks and introductory courses. However, the "ideal" is ever changing and the evolutionary process is ongoing. A follow-up study which is directed toward basic courses in accounting beyond the introductory course is currently being conducted by the American Accounting Association.

Continuing Education

Of fundamental importance is recognition by all concerned that education is a lifelong process. No field of knowledge is static. Changes in the environment are so frequent that one author has coined the phrase *future shock* to describe a current social malady. Today's college graduates may find themselves obsolete ten years from now if they fail to continue their studies.

The trend seems to be, therefore, for accounting courses at the universities to be designed and conducted so as to stimulate the students' intellectual curiosity and to instill habits of independent reading and research. This is not an easy task at best, but it becomes almost impossible if students are unresponsive. A sustained ability for self-learning has been called one of the primary objectives of formal education. But it can hardly be taught. In trying to cultivate this ability, a student simply has to take the initiative.

The opportunities for continuing education after college are proliferating. Corporations, management associations, governmental agencies, accounting firms, and professional accounting societies conduct training sessions and seminars on a wide variety of subjects, at levels ranging from elementary to advanced. Universities offer extension courses, noncredit courses in residence, and adult education programs. Correspondence schools offer instruction by mail. An abundant literature on accounting and all areas of management is available to the individual who is willing to study it.

Impact of the CPA Examination

The CPA examination has undoubtedly had a strong influence on accounting education. Since the CPA certificate has been the only visible identification of professional competence in accounting until recent years, some students who majored in this subject expected their courses to prepare them to meet the CPA requirements. Many accounting faculties took pride in the numbers of their students who became certified public accountants and especially in those who won medals for high marks on the CPA examination.

Inevitably, textbooks were heavily weighted with subject matter often dealt with in the examinations. Problem materials for classroom use were conveniently available from past CPA examinations.

However, as pointed out earlier, the CPA examination was historically oriented strongly to the independent audit of financial statements. It was presumed that candidates had experience in public accounting, and the examination was regarded as a test of competence for the practice of public accounting. This practice, in turn, originally consisted largely of independent audits, assistance in preparation of financial statements and tax returns, and installation of financial accounting systems.

But times have changed. Management advisory services have taken a larger place in the range of services offered by public accounting firms. And an increasing number of CPAs have occupied executive positions in business and government. While financial reporting and independent auditing have become more important than ever—both to managers and to public accountants—the accounting needs of managers as a basis for planning, control, and decision making have demanded a rapidly increasing share of attention in academic, practicing, and research circles.

The CPA and the CMA examinations have been responding to these changes. For example, the CPA examination may be expected to include questions and problems requiring understanding of computers, statistical sampling, budgeting, forecasting, capital budgeting, cost accounting, price-level adjustments, quantitative methods and techniques, mathematics, statistics, and probability—all this, of course, in addition to the more familiar areas of financial accounting, auditing, and income taxation. A basic knowledge of economics and finance and an ability to write clear English are assumed. No doubt in the years ahead additional subjects will be included. The changes must be gradual, since the examination cannot reasonably cover subjects in which instruction is not yet generally available. Changes in curricula are also likely to be made gradually, as new teaching materials become available.

Professional Ethics

Integrity on the part of professional people is at least as important as technical competence. Those who rely on professional accountants usually cannot evaluate the quality of the service rendered. They do not understand accounting well enough, or they would not have to rely on others. Therefore, those who put their faith in accountants have a right to expect they will be served not only competently but also honestly and fairly.

To provide assurance to the public that this expectation will be justified, the accounting profession, like all professions, has established a code of ethics, the violation of which may result in reprimand, suspension, or expulsion of the offending member. The code has evolved over more than half a century, becoming ever more explicit and ever more rigorous as the profession matured and as the public expected it to assume greater responsibilities.

Originally, the ethical rules focused only on the conduct of certified public accountants in their capacity as independent auditors. It was in this area that the need to maintain public confidence was most urgent, since not only clients but also investors, creditors, and others relied on the representations of independent auditors. Later, however, the code was expanded to cover tax practice and management advisory services, and recently ethical standards for CPAs employed in industry have been suggested. The code of professional ethics was restated in 1972 and covers rules dealing with five broad principles:

Independence, Integrity, and Objectivity   In the practice of public accounting CPAs should refuse to subordinate their judgments to those of others, including clients, and should express their conclusions honestly and objectively. In addition, when acting as independent auditors, they should avoid relationships likely to raise doubts as to their impartiality in the minds of reasonable observers; for example, CPAs are prohibited from having a financial interest in, or serving as officers or directors of, corporations of which they are independent auditors.

Competence and Technical Standards   A CPA should conform with the technical standards established by the profession; for example, the generally accepted accounting principles and auditing standards described in Chapters 4 and 5. Furthermore, CPAs should not undertake any engagement in any area of practice in which they are not competent to perform at an acceptable level of professionalism.

Responsibilities to Clients CPAs should have a sincere concern for their clients' interests consistent with their responsibilities to the public. They should hold in strict confidence information about a client's affairs acquired in the course of their engagement. They should not exploit the relationship with a client for personal advantage; for example, a CPA is prohibited from accepting a commission for referring the seller of a product or service to the client. However, they should be frank and straightforward with clients and, if necessary, resign when irreconcilable differences arise on questions of principle.

Responsibilities to Colleagues CPAs should conduct themselves in a manner that will encourage cooperation and good relations among members of the profession. A CPA should not seek to displace another accountant in a client relationship. CPAs should support the professional societies and help ensure universal compliance with the code of ethics. They should assist other practitioners when requested and should call on them for help when needed.

Other Responsibilities and Practices The code prohibits advertising and solicitation, certain types of promotional practices, and publicity inspired by the CPA. CPAs may not engage in an occupation incompatible with their public accounting practice, such as selling insurance or securities. They should conduct themselves personally in a manner that will enhance public respect and confidence.

These general standards of conduct are supported by detailed rules and official interpretations, departures from which may result in formal trial and disciplinary action by the professional societies of certified public accountants. The penalties can be severe: expulsion from professional societies, revocation of the CPA certificate by state authorities, loss of right to represent clients before the Internal Revenue Service, exclusion from audits of financial statements filed with the

Securities and Exchange Commission. Penalties of this severity, of course, result only from serious offenses and are rare. Violations of less significance are usually corrected by reprimand or warning.

While the ethics committees are busy and trial boards meet frequently to hear complaints, the record of CPAs as a whole is extraordinarily good. Cases of dishonesty or deliberate deception are so infrequent as to be almost negligible in relation to the numbers of CPAs in practice and the volume of professional engagements performed. The majority of complaints stem from ignorance, carelessness, or poor judgment on the part of the offenders. And even these constitute only an infinitesimal percentage of the total volume.

The foregoing applies mainly to certified public accountants engaged in public accounting, that is, those who offer their services to the public on a fee basis rather than those who are employed full-time. It was for the former that the code was originally designed, as noted earlier. But tens of thousands of CPAs hold positions in industry and government, and the question has arisen whether they too have ethical responsibilities as members of the accounting profession. The present code makes no specific reference to them, but some think it should.

CPAs who are controllers or financial vice presidents of corporations, for example, obviously owe primary loyalty to their employers. Situations may arise, however, when they may wonder whether this loyalty is due only to the president of the company or to the board of directors or to the stockholders as a whole. At present, the profession offers no definite guidelines.

Dishonesty or deliberate deception is rare among CPAs in industry as among those in public practice. But there are countless questions requiring delicate judgments involved in financial reporting and determination of income taxes, for example, on which differences of opinion may arise within the management team. Certain disclosures, for instance, might be helpful to individual stockholders as investors but possibly damaging to the competitive position of the company as a whole. The point at which a CPA-executive should assert his independence even from his employers is difficult enough to decide, but the question is complicated by the fact that management accountants who are not CPAs would not be bound by any ethical code that might be applied to the CPAs.

On the other hand, it can be argued that by serving the public interest to the best of their ability, management accountants will also be serving the best interest of their employers, since in the long run—perhaps even in the short run— the companies most likely to prosper are those having full confidence of investors, creditors, tax authorities, regulatory agencies, labor unions, the financial press, and the community generally. Accounting and financial reporting can play a significant part in generating such confidence.

There is evidence that many CPAs in industry would welcome authoritative guidance as to their ethical responsibilities, and perhaps the professional societies of which many of them are members will see fit to provide it.

Social Obligations

Professional accountants are keenly conscious of their social obligations. Their earnest concern with ethical questions, their preoccupation with refinement of accounting principles and auditing procedures, their voluntary delineation of their own responsibilities in tax practice, their strong support of accounting research and education, are all sufficient evidence of awareness of their responsibility to society.

The social contribution of accountants has already been described in Chapter 1. It is sometimes assumed that social contribution is synonymous with volunteer work undertaken outside of office hours. But, in fact, the greatest service accountants can render to society—as can lawyers, doctors, engineers, architects, or any professional people—is to do a good job in the daily work for which they get paid.

On top of this, however, accountants accept the responsibilities of all good citizens. They participate in community affairs by the tens of thousands. They accept public office in local, state, and federal governments, often at a financial sacrifice. They contribute money to charity and education. They strive for minority opportunity in the profession. Individually, through their firms and corporations and through the professional societies, they offer aid to minority business executives, advice on urban problems, grants to black colleges, scholarships to disadvantaged students, and help to the emerging accounting profession in developing countries.

This young and dynamic profession tries to do everything that might be expected of it. It incessantly searches for ways to improve the quality of its service and for channels through which to extend its services more widely. The likelihood of success in both directions will be discussed in Chapter 9, which deals with the outlook for the future.

Summary

Like everything else associated with modern accounting, its attainment of professional status has occurred in a remarkably short time. The same development in law and medicine took place over centuries. Accounting in the United States has satisfied the five criteria of a profession within the last fifty years, although a start was made some twenty-five years earlier.

Even now the process can be said to be incomplete, since not all accountants engaged at a professional level are charged with a social obligation or are governed by a code of ethics or have satisfied formal requirements and obtained an identifying title or have acquired the entire body of specialized knowledge or have obtained legal recognition.

But thousands have done so, and thousands more are preparing to meet all these criteria. And trends are in motion giving reason to hope that in time all professional accountants will have met the same standards and will be united under one banner.

Discussion Questions

1   Why is accounting considered a profession?
2   Explain why it was primarily the auditing function which forced professional accounting standards into being.
3   Why is the development of a code of ethics so vital to accountants?

4 Why have management consulting or management advisory services become a more important and extensive service of accounting firms?

5 What basic change in accounting education has occurred recently?

6 In what directions are the educational requirements for accountants headed in the future?

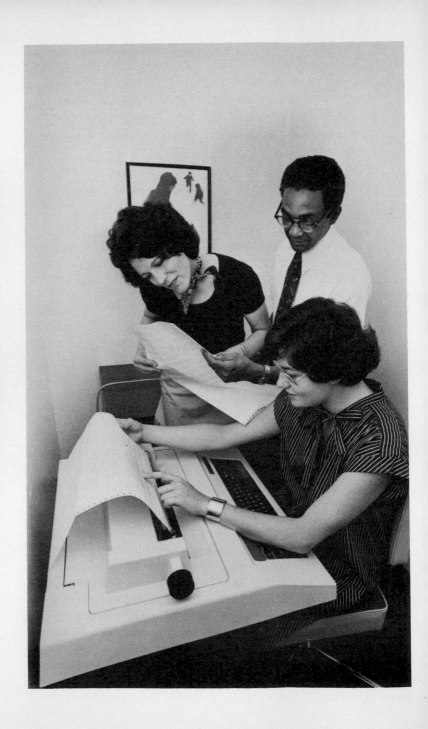

9
Outlook for the Future

With every tick of the clock a part of the future slides into the past. In human affairs what is going to happen is inevitably related to what has already happened. What people are thinking about, exploring, researching, and experimenting with today is quite likely to become reality tomorrow.

In the accounting profession there are trends already in motion that strongly suggest a vast expansion of the role of accounting in the next decade. Thus, in considering the future, it is necessary to discuss some possibilities already alluded to in earlier chapters.

In considering the future, it is useful to think of accounting broadly as a network of information reaching in all directions and channeled to all centers where decisions are made involving the allocation of resources. No longer is it assumed that accounting deals only with what has happened in the past—facts. It clearly deals also with future probabilities using the past as a guide to the future. No longer, either, is it assumed that accounting is confined to information that can be presented with mathematical precision. Clearly, it involves estimates and judgments.

The information accounting provides is packaged in many different forms and arrangements, in greater or lesser detail, so as to be most useful to the various users to which it is directed. It may cover the activities of an entire organization or only one part of the activities of one segment of an organization.

No longer should it be assumed that accounting deals only with money. It deals also with quantities expressed in nonfinancial terms. It deals, too, with organizational structures, systems, and procedures through which assets are safeguarded, costs are minimized, and sound decisions reached.

In everything it does accounting must conform with legal requirements involving property rights, corporate powers, taxation, and governmental regulations.

With these generalizations in mind, it is easier to envisage the probable expansion of the role of accounting in the years ahead: first, in the traditional areas of financial reporting and auditing; second, in the field of managerial accounting; third, in the more esoteric realm identified as "social accounting"; and finally, in the area of accounting education. In all these areas the profession is faced with challenges that sooner or later will result in changes.

Financial Reporting

Despite the marked improvements in the financial reports of business enterprises over the past forty years—improvements which have been accelerated in the past twenty years—there is still much discontent. Some of it suggests the need for radical change.

The basic financial statements—balance sheets, income statements, statements of changes in financial position—do not lend themselves, it has been alleged, to an adequate description of the highly complex affairs of the modern business corporation. The traditional statements, it is true, were originally designed for simple trading firms and later for relatively simple manufacturing firms. While these statements have been elaborated and supplemented with explanatory footnotes and summaries, their essential structure remains unchanged. Generally accepted accounting principles have developed within this structure, which some critics regard as too confining for modern needs. It has been said, for example, that efforts to "shoehorn" complex economic realities into the confines of what critics regard as an inadequate structure are doomed to failure.

Ranges   Various innovations have been suggested. One is the use of ranges, reflecting tolerances in the reliability of estimates. Instead of a single precise figure indicating earnings per share, for example, some critics suggest indicating a range between the most optimistic and the most pessimistic probabilities, based on possible variations in estimates of depreciation, losses from bad debts, termination of contracts, tax adjustments, and other events whose impact cannot immediately be determined precisely but which affect reported income. This proposal probably will not be received with enthusiasm by corporate managements or by some accountants, but it opens up an interesting field for research and experimentation, which could in time lead to some changes.

Bookkeeping Constraints Complaint is made also that the rigor of double-entry bookkeeping, on which the traditional financial statements are based, requires every expenditure to be recorded either as an increase in assets or as a current expense. But it is claimed that expenditures for research, advertising, and personnel development, for example, are not easy to classify in either category at the time they are made. Arbitrary decisions could mislead investors and credit grantors.

Uncertainties Some observers urge that it would be much better to identify clearly the uncertainties in financial statements, which are, in fact, the uncertainties inherent in economic realities, than to encourage users of such statements to believe that precision and total accuracy are possible in economic affairs.

All-purpose Statements In any event, there is mounting opinion that the so-called all-purpose financial statements—the familiar balance sheet, income statement, and statement of change in financial position—do not effectively serve the needs of various users. Bankers who lend other people's money, for example, are concerned mainly about the availability of cash for repayment of the loans, and they want information on which they can judge the risk of loss. Stockholders, however, are more interested in the trend of earnings and the possibilities of growth. Regulatory agencies, labor unions, consumer groups, all have special information requirements. Different forms of financial statements, and even different accounting principles, for different purposes may be developed in response to public pressures.

Investigation of the needs and desires of different users of financial statements is already a popular area of accounting research and will likely be expanded in the future.

Forecasts Proposals for the publication of forecasts of operations and capital investment are increasing. While there is a natural reluctance to take responsibility for predictions of future events, it has been pointed out that even conventional financial statements for annual periods are significantly based on probabilities. In reality, economic activities are a continuous stream; they do not cease at the end of a year and start afresh on the first day of the new year. Investors would like to have management's best judgment, soundly based, on its plans for the year or two ahead as well as comparative results for a number of years past, which are now widely published.

Price Levels and Current Values Reference has been made earlier to the pressures for price-level accounting, taking note of the erosion of the purchasing power of the currency because of inflation. For several years recommendations have been made that price-level adjusted supplementary statements be published along with the traditional statements, but not many companies have so reported. This is still a topic under consideration by the Financial Accounting Standards Board. There is also increased pressure, especially from the SEC, to disclose the current values of inventories and other assets, which is even a step beyond price-level adjustments.

Disclosures More disclosure is being demanded by financial analysts, bankers, and other users of financial information. They would like to know a company's backlog of orders, for example, detailed operating results of the different segments of a large and diverse enterprise, and the results of specific investments in new ventures or acquisitions of existing companies. They would like to have breakdowns of research expenditures and a separation of administrative and selling expenses. Managements tend to resist such proposals on the ground that such information would help competitors.

The usual response is that if all companies whose securities are widely held agreed to comply, or were required to do so, they would be on an equal competitive footing. But this would not prevent foreign companies selling products here from gaining an unfair advantage over their American competitors, unless some way were found to compel the foreign concerns to make similar disclosures and open their own countries' market to American penetration.

Leases One specific disclosure item which has been debated extensively for several years is leases. Traditionally, leases have not been recorded on the books but have been disclosed in footnotes to financial statements, if at all. Requirements are now imminent which will make it mandatory to report as assets and liabilities any leases meeting certain criteria. This will have a significant impact on companies heavily involved in leasing activities.

Comparability The pressure for greater comparability of reported earnings, discussed in Chapter 4, is likely to increase. It will require more efforts to define, refine, and perhaps modify generally accepted accounting principles.

Not only has the number of stockholders increased significantly in recent years, but also the level of their sophistication is rising rapidly as well. The bulk of transactions on the New York Stock Exchange originate with institutions that retain expert financial analysts as advisors—pension funds, mutual funds, foundations, endowment funds, investment bankers, and so on. Even individual investors have the advice of researchers employed by brokers and access to countless investment services. The professional analysts are fully aware of the significance of financial reporting and are vocal in their criticism of what they believe to be its shortcomings. To the extent that their reasonable needs can be met, it must be assumed that in time they will be.

Social Expenditures New dimensions may be added to financial reporting by increasing emphasis on the social responsibilities of business enterprises. It has already been pointed out that reporting standards must be developed for costs incurred by companies in altering their processes or their products to eliminate pollution of the environment. These costs will be passed on to consumers, or to stockholders (via lower profits), or to taxpayers (via government subsidies), but the rate and the period of time over which they will be passed on are interesting accounting questions.

Corporations are also being urged to participate in efforts to improve the quality of life generally, not only by financial support of education and the arts but also by contribution of their managerial and technical know-how to public problem solving; for example, prevention of urban deterioration, training and placement of hard-core unemployed, recycling of waste materials, preservation of natural environment. Many companies have been active in these areas, and some are spending additional money to advertise their concern for the quality of life.

Expenditures for purposes of this kind may be difficult to associate directly with the production of net income. It has been suggested publicly that in addition to the regular financial statements, certified by independent accountants, corporations may submit to a "social audit," resulting in statements, similarly certified, reflecting the companies' contributions in manpower, materials, equipment, and money to improvement of the quality of life.

The FASB and SEC   Changes in financial reporting requirements, such as those mentioned, will likely come as a result of specific pronouncements by the Financial Accounting Standards Board and the Securities and Exchange Commission. Both of these standard-setting bodies have been extremely active in recent years in terms of the number of new reporting requirements established. If anything, this activity is likely to increase in the foreseeable future, making financial reporting changes the rule, not the exception.

Auditing

Auditing and financial reporting are virtually inseparable. A competent, independent review of the financial representations made by those in charge of any activity is almost essential to avoid a credibility gap.

If changes in financial reporting discussed in the preceding section are adopted, the independent auditor will be asked to express a professional opinion as to whether the additional information is fairly presented. This will broaden the already widening scope of the auditors' responsibilities and will involve consideration of potential legal liability.

Forecasts As implied in Chapter 5, uncertainties as to the extent of the auditor's legal liability inevitably deter innovation and experimentation. For example, suppose a public accounting firm reports that in its opinion a forecast of future sales, expenses, and net income is reasonable, based on past experience, all available current evidence, and a study of relevant economic trends. Then unforeseen events prove the forecast to be materially wrong. Will the accounting firm be sued for millions of dollars by investors who claim they lost money by relying on the accountants' opinion? If so, what would the courts decide? Court decisions on accountants' liability in connection with conventional financial statements have seemed to many observers unnecessarily severe. They do not encourage assumption of additional risks.

Yet the users of financial statements clearly would like the independent auditor to take on more responsibility: to provide assurance that the accounting principles followed and the disclosures provided reflect the economic realities; to provide a professional, unbiased, educated guess about the future, as well as a record of the past; and to indicate whether the internal accounting and control procedures are effective enough to prevent unpleasant surprises.

Internal Control On this last point a cautious step forward has already been taken, as mentioned briefly in Chapter 5. The national organization of certified public accountants has issued a form of report that independent auditors may use for reporting their evaluations of internal control.

As explained, the auditor must study clients' internal controls in order to determine the extent to which reliance may be placed on the financial records and the extent to which audit tests, samples, confirmations, and physical observation must be undertaken. Knowing this, bankers, financial analysts, and governmental agencies have asked for the auditor's opinion as to whether internal controls are adequate or not.

In the form of report recommended, it is emphasized that internal controls cannot provide absolute assurance against loss or absolute reliability of financial records—only *reasonable* assurance. Limitations on the potential effectiveness of any system of internal control are described. With additional reservations as to the extent of the auditor's responsibility, the report finally states what the auditor believes to be material weaknesses in the control system or that no such weaknesses came to light.

Furthermore, it is recommended that auditors' reports on internal control be furnished on request to management and regulatory agencies, and under appropriate conditions to other independent auditors. However, they should not be released to the general public, including investors and credit grantors, unless management or a regulatory agency having jurisdiction chooses to do so.

This extremely cautious approach to an extension of the auditor's service for which there is evidence of public demand is clearly guided by recognition of a potential legal liability of indeterminate extent. It is a good illustration of how legal uncertainty inhibits the accounting profession from moving forward with confidence into new areas of service.

No one objects to suitable punishment for deliberate fraud, intentional deception, or gross carelessness. But under existing legal precedents an accounting firm could be wiped out financially by making an honest error of judgment or an unintentional mistake in procedure. Millions of dollars have been paid out to satisfy claims against accounting firms in cases where their fees were only in the tens of thousands. Some limitation of the amounts for which auditors are liable to the countless users who may rely on their reports is essential if the accounting profession is to give the public the best service of which it is capable. Such protection might be provided by the courts, the Securities and Exchange Commission, or legislation.

Information Systems Among other extensions of audit services that have been suggested is the expression of opinion on the adequacy of the client's entire information system: Does it provide what the client needs both for planning and decision making and for external reporting? Is its cost reasonable in relation to its usefulness? The auditor, already familiar with a client's organizational structure, procedures, and financial affairs, is normally in a good position to extend an investigation sufficiently to answer these questions. Public accountants have always designed information systems, and they still do. A formal report to management on the adequacy of its system would be a valuable addition to the audit service, and of particular interest to boards of directors.

Management Audits   Further out in the spectrum of future opportunities for auditors is the audit of management performance. It is recognized that financial results alone do not necessarily reflect good management: They do not show how much better the results might have been. Neither do they indicate the internal strengths or weaknesses of an organization, which may have a bearing on future financial results.

Speculation about the possibility of establishing standards, procedures, and forms of reports for audits of management performance has appeared in a number of professional publications. Among the types of questions to which such an audit might seek answers are the following—by no means a complete list:

How do the company's ratios of operating earnings to sales and of operating earning to long-term capital investment compare with the return earned by the industry as a whole?

How does the rate of growth compare with those of similar companies?

Is the information system adequate?

Are controls up to modern standards?

Are planning and decision-making procedures up to modern standards?

Are personnel and labor relations reasonably satisfactory?

Is there an acceptable executive development program and a satisfactory plan for succession to top management positions?

Are expenditures for research and development excessive or inadequate?

Do expenditures for advertising and promotion appear to be sufficiently productive?

Are the pension plan and other fringe benefit provisions adequate in terms of new and continually changing federal and state requirements?

These are only a few of the questions that might be asked. It is assumed that formal audit programs would have to be developed and that audit or administrative service teams would include management specialists as well as financial accountants.

The formal audit of management performance for public information may be far in the future, if indeed it has any future at all, but the increasing literature on the subject suggests that some experimental steps toward this objective, for management's own benefit, are likely to be made before long. Corporate boards of directors might consider even a partial, informal review of this nature as a protection to themselves against criticism.

The Computer   Any discussion of the future of auditing must include reference to the computer, which affects every aspect of accounting. In Chapter 5 it was noted that computerization of accounting systems will probably reduce the detailed audit work necessary when masses of documentation must be reviewed. Consequently, audit staffs may be reduced in relative number, but will require personnel of increasingly high-quality training.

The continuing rapid expansion of the capacities of computers will also require changes in familiar auditing techniques, especially in the evaluation of internal controls, the importance of which has already been discussed.

Computers are available that permit introduction of accounting information from remote points directly into the central processing unit. Programs or systems are stored within the computer, which automatically processes the data thus introduced. Familiar paper "audit trails," such as ledgers and journals, will tend to disappear. Correspondingly, the need for the development of computer audit trails will increase.

Furthermore, in large-scale information systems the computer will receive not only accounting data but also other types of information needed by management.

Broadly speaking, human intervention in the *processing* of the data tends to be eliminated. A few people control the instructions lodged in the computer and the data currently introduced.

Testing the validity of the controls and evaluating the reliability of the information produced by the system confront auditors with new and difficult problems. They are not insoluble, but they will require a reorientation to unfamiliar circumstances and sufficient technical understanding of computer operations to enable auditors to satisfy themselves that the controls are adequate.

Managerial Accounting

Not only as auditors are accountants affected by the continuing computer revolution. It is predicted that manual record keeping and data processing will soon disappear as computers become readily available and increasingly economical even for use by smaller organizations.

Controllers, financial vice presidents, and internal accounting staffs, as well as public accountants, may be threatened by obsolescence if they do not understand the ways in which computers may be used. These now include preparation of tax returns, cash management, inventory control, payroll accounting, and other functions of a more or less routine nature.

More important and more fascinating are the increasingly sophisticated approaches to decision making that the computer makes possible. Brief reference was made in Chapter 6 to the use of "models" in managerial planning and decision making. In this context a model has been described as a representation of a real or probable situation encompassing all known significant factors in meaningful relations (such as cost, price, return on investment). Models can be used to reveal the probable effects of varying assumptions, based on the best available information, concerning the combination of factors that will produce the best results.

The use of such models is already fairly standard procedure

in many large organizations that have computers available. In the future, competition is likely to require that all organizations use them as accepted tools of competent management. But without access to computers, the clerical cost of creating, for instance, as many as twenty models based on varying assumptions in order to make a single decision, and repeating the process to monitor the effectiveness of the decision once made, would be prohibitive.

On a larger scale, if the budget is regarded as a model of financial results for a given time period, the computer makes it possible to correct the budget continuously as actual events vary from original estimates. Again, the clerical cost of such continuous budgeting without the computer would be prohibitively high.

These are only illustrations of an almost infinite range of possible applications of computers in planning, control, and decision making. They can be the repositories of comprehensive information systems; they can process masses of data at high speeds and low costs; they can produce financial statements, tax returns, and special reports in obedience to programmed instructions; and they can produce decision models that would be prohibitively costly by manual means.

Accountants of the future—beginning tomorrow—must understand the uses and the technology of these machines or run the risk of finding their professional activities severely limited.

Management Information   It has been mentioned earlier that accounting for managerial planning, control, and decision making began to take form as a structured body of theory somewhat later than so-called financial accounting.

However, progress in management accounting has been rapid, and it is predicted that in the relatively near future a unified body of accepted theory in this field will have emerged. Participation in this development will be a stimulating experience for many accountants.

Until recently, management accounting, like financial accounting and auditing at the turn of the century, was essentially pragmatic. A series of techniques such as budgeting and cost accounting was aimed at specific management problems, but they were not necessarily integrated within a theoretical framework. New knowledge, the availability of the computer, and adaptations of mathematics, however, are accelerating movement toward a unifying conceptual foundation.

The process involves systematic analysis of the decisions that managements of all types of organizations are required to make, then a study of the information needed as a basis for each type of decision, and finally the design of systems providing the needed information. Much of this information, incidentally, might be external to the operations of the organization itself. For example, capital budgeting might require information on markets and competitors' shares of them. Product-line decisions should take into account changing consumer tastes and habits. Internal-control decisions involve organizational structure, such as the composition of cost centers, which may require consideration of behavioral patterns (this will be discussed later in the chapter), and so on.

The increasing importance of nonprofit organizations in the economy—notably government—increases the need for development of a theoretical framework for management accounting to serve as a basis for specific systems designed for the purposes of individual organizations.

It is already widely recognized that accounting principles accepted for financial reporting purposes may not be most useful for special reports to management. For example, so-called current-value accounting, which isolates the effect of current costs on inventories, may be more useful to management than accounting based on historical cost, which, up to the present at least, is the only basis consistent with generally accepted accounting principles. This suggests that principles or methods developed for managerial purposes may in some instances prove superior for financial reports to outsiders also and may displace those currently accepted. The close interrelation between management accounting and financial accounting would thus be emphasized.

Cost-Benefit Relations Passing reference to cost-benefit relations was made in earlier chapters. In profit-making organizations the net income and increase in owners' equity are accepted as evidence that benefit justified cost. Conventional accounting reports, however, do not reveal whether costs were too high and net income therefore too low; whether specific decisions, such as acquisition of another business, investment in a new plant, or launching of a new product, resulted in unnecessary losses; or, on the other hand, whether opportunities for profitable activities were neglected.

Accountants are studying techniques of information analysis that may provide answers to such questions, which progressive managements will welcome. It is, however, in the area of nonprofit activities that the cost-benefit relation presents newer and more difficult problems.

Membership organizations such as professional societies and trade associations can make a stab at costing their activities by allocating salaries and overhead to specific projects (though very few of them do). By questionnaires they can determine in a general way which services their members consider of most value. Management can then decide which activities are worth what they cost and which are not. There is a wide field for useful service by accountants in improving the financial management of membership and other nonprofit organizations.

Social Accounting

Of overriding social importance, however, is the determination of cost-benefit relations in social programs financed by government, foundation grants, or charitable organizations.

As government, particularly, becomes committed to programs in such areas as health, education, welfare, and defense, which cost many billions of dollars, it is of vital importance to all citizens to know whether the benefits are really worth the sacrifices required of the taxpayers who are the principal source of governmental funds.

There are limits to the resources of even this affluent nation. Ruinous inflation can be the result of overspending. Establishment of priorities is a critical need. And for this, accounting information is essential.

But how can the results of social programs be measured? Determining the costs is not difficult. But putting a dollar value on the product of a program to eliminate illiteracy or to improve public health is another matter.

However, there have been experiments that promise possible solutions. Perhaps measurement devices other than dollars can be used to appraise results. For example, accountants participated in a project to compare the effectiveness of two approaches to the education of school children of the same age. Tests, administered by educators, measuring a child's academic ability in comparison with scores of a large number of children of the same age were utilized. By testing each child in the experimental group at the beginning and at the end of the term, a reasonably reliable indicator of progress was obtained. The accountants determined the costs of the two programs, including teachers' compensation, equipment, textbooks, and other costs. One program proved superior to the other, and its costs were not excessive.

The accounting profession is fully aware of the needs and opportunities in cost-benefit analysis and is exploring ways in which it can help in providing solutions. An accounting firm helped measure traffic patterns in a populous section as part of a study to determine where and how federal transportation funds could be spent most effectively, not only in terms of speeding up transportation but also in terms of improving the environment for residents of the area.

Another accounting firm helped to determine the most effective use of welfare funds in a large city. Others have participated in studies of the public use of state parks, wildlife patterns in game preserves, and water and air pollution in two states.

It should be emphasized that in all such studies accountants cooperated with experts in other disciplines. It would be absurd to suggest that any one discipline could deal with such complex problems alone.

It may be predicted that cost-benefit analysis in nonprofit activities will be one of the major challenges and opportunities facing accountants in the years ahead.

Human Reactions to Accounting

Another trend in accounting is to pay more attention to the relationship of accounting to people. One reason for this is recognition that accountants deal with formal organizations. The behavior of individuals who comprise formal organizations is of primary concern to management. The information accountants provide to managements will be most useful if it takes into account personal motivations, reactions to unfamiliar situations, resistance to change, and other common characteristics.

As pointed out briefly in Chapter 6, this is why the behavioral sciences like psychology and sociology are recommended as part of the accounting curriculum in college.

But not much has been done yet by the profession itself to adapt its traditional procedures to the needs, attitudes, and capacities of the people who are intended to use the information accounting provides. This is a rich field for research and for the implementation of research findings in the immediate future.

Much is being written on the subject. For example, it has been pointed out that many individuals in sizable organizations receive accounting information to aid them in planning, budgeting, directing, and controlling their activities. Accountants may continue to assume that economic gain for the enterprise and financial incentive for the individual are organizational and personal goals. However, it is now increasingly accepted that a person's needs are not only physical but also psychological. To be sure, people want enough money to assure reasonable comfort, but they also need a sense of security, the affection of other people, and a feeling that they are respected and are using their abilities to good purpose.

The question is whether the way the accountant "keeps score" helps to reinforce an obsolete approach to management: Does accounting serve as a constraint on management's ability to change its policies with respect to human motivation? Specifically, budgets, the structure of cost centers, internal-reporting requirements, cost controls, audits, and internal-control systems must have a positive effect on employee attitudes. How can that effect be most constructive? Perhaps the orientation of accounting should be changed from discipline, control, restraint, and strict accountability to support of individual employees in their respective tasks.

The reactions of people outside the organization to financial reports—that is, creditors, stockholders, members, taxpayers, labor unions, consumers, and so on—are of vital importance to business organizations in particular and to many nonprofit organizations as well. Yet little is known about whether such reports communicate what the issuers intend; whether the recipients feel they are getting the information they need; whether the reports are useful as guides to action; or whether they encourage confidence, suspicion, or hostility.

Some research on these questions is being undertaken, but much more is likely in the near future. The findings might influence significant changes in the content of financial statements and auditors' reports or opinions.

Accounting for Human Resources

Organizations are composed of people. The effectiveness of these people determines the relative success of organizations in achieving their objectives. Consequently, a highly effective group of managers and employees is one of the most valuable assets an organization can possess—one might argue, the most valuable. The most modern plant and machinery, the newest computer, or the most elaborate plans will not make an organization successful if its people are incompetent, lazy, or poorly motivated. Yet this highly important asset does not appear on any balance sheet, nor does the customary income statement reflect the impact of greater or fewer expenditures to increase the effectiveness of an organization's people.

Accountants, mainly those in academic circles, are beginning to study ways of evaluating human resources, but as yet no one has discovered a technique whereby a dollar amount can be applied to them. The problem is important, however, to managements and to investors and creditors. Management would like to know how its human resources compare with those of similar organizations. Investors and creditors would like to know whether the effectiveness of management and employees is likely to be sustained in the years ahead.

For example, a company may flourish for years under a brilliant executive, but there may be no one trained to succeed that individual upon retirement. On the other hand, a company in trouble may continue to show good earnings for a few years by ruthlessly firing people, abandoning training programs, and impairing morale of workers by harsh supervisory practices. But the end results may be disastrous.

A company may report lower earnings than some competitors because it chooses to spend more money in building up its human resources for continuous growth of the organization. This can be done by careful recruiting of superior personnel, by good personnel administration, by training programs, and by arrangements assuring the presence of competent successors to incumbents of all key managerial and supervisory positions. These activities are quite costly, but they represent a sound investment in the future.

Yet investors rarely receive information enabling them to distinguish among the several possible situations. If investors rely wholly on earnings per share, they may choose a company that may be heading downhill, while a company showing more modest current net income may be likely to grow and prosper.

Perhaps a partial remedy would be disclosure of expenditures on improvement of human resources in comparison with those of earlier years. This would at least indicate whether the "value" of the human-resources asset was going up or down, although even this indication might not be conclusive.

It has been said that for centuries accountants have been measuring the productivity of human resources, but now there is need to measure the extent of investment in these resources. Ultimately, accountants are likely to develop sophisticated techniques permitting additional standards of reporting on human resources to be formulated.

Accounting Education

As indicated by the areas of increased financial disclosures, additional audit responsibilities, expansion of managerial accounting techniques, and new applications of social accounting, the accountant of tomorrow needs more extensive education and training. Not only are there more topics to be covered, but the level of competency required is increasing because of higher expectations of accountants by the public.

The result is a movement toward five-year professional schools of accountancy. In the future it may be that a four-year formal educational experience will not be considered adequate for preparing students to enter the accounting profession. A committee of the American Institute of CPAs is already on record as favoring a five-year college education requirement for certification of public accountants. The AICPA has also endorsed the establishment of professional schools of accounting at qualified and receptive universities.

To meet the expanding challenges in accounting, educational programs will be required to trim coverage of less relevant topics and expand coverage of other topics, such as the interaction of the legal and government environment with accounting, the obligations and attitudinal training of professional accountants, the communication skill requirements of the professional accountant, and many more.

In addition to business and accounting core requirements needed by all who would be qualified for entrance to the accounting profession, it is likely that emphasis will be placed upon specialization in areas such as auditing, taxation, management advisory services, managerial accounting, and non-profit accounting. The challenge to accounting education in the future is to keep pace with the dynamic changes and expanding professional opportunities in accounting.

Summary

This chapter does not purport to be a comprehensive or a detailed assessment of all aspects of the accounting profession's outlook for the future.

Among notable omissions is the probable participation of accountants in preparation of national income and balance of payments accounts. The growing trend toward internationalism in business and finance also raises problems and opportunities for accountants (including foreign travel for individual accountants).

But enough has been said to indicate the rapidly expanding range of interests and scope of opportunities for accountants. Two significant patterns seem to emerge. First, public interest in accounting and recognition of the contributions it can make are on the rise. Consequently, the levels of influence and authority at which accountants operate are constantly rising also. Second, interdisciplinary approaches to complex managerial, economic, and social problems are increasing. More and more, accountants will find themselves working with lawyers, economists, mathematicians, sociologists, and other experts.

Specialization is also a likely development; indeed, in many instances it has already occurred. An accounting background combined with law, economics, mathematics, computer technology, or other disciplines may enable an individual to undertake highly specialized tasks. And within the field of accounting itself there is a significant demand for specialists.

Whatever the future of accounting may hold, it will not be boring. It may not be relaxing either!

Discussion Questions

1   What are some possible future developments in the field of financial reporting?

2   Why are costs, such as those for research and advertising, hard to classify in terms of expense or asset categories?

3   What are some of the arguments favoring a greater variety of accounting reports covering a wider range of needs?

4   Why is a cost-benefit analysis of social programs so difficult to prepare?

5   If human assets are admittedly the most valuable asset of a firm, why are they the least accounted for?

6   What is there about the nature of accounting that is causing it to spread and expand its scope into many new fields?

10

Careers in Professional Accounting

Accounting as a profession has existed in the United States for less than one hundred years. However, about half that time was spent in struggles by relatively small numbers of men and women to establish effective organizations, develop standards, create a professional literature, and seek public recognition.

Broadly speaking, professional accountants have been widely organized and accepted as such for little more than forty years, and then principally by segments of the public directly interested in their work—bankers, investors, business executives, lawyers, governmental agencies, and so on.

Meanwhile, the title *accountant* was freely assumed by individuals who made no claim to professional status, but who were engaged in record keeping or other more or less routine tasks required as part of the basic accounting function.

It is not surprising, therefore, that the words *accounting* and *accountant* have conveyed to a large segment of the general public an impression of highly technical but repetitive, routine work involving a lot of pencil pushing. This impression is rapidly disappearing, but it persists to some extent, even on university campuses.

Readers of this book should have no difficulty in dismissing any such lingering impression about *professional* accounting. The opportunities and rewards available to professional accountants are second to none. They are at least equal, in terms of both remuneration and useful social service, to those of corporate managers, high governmental officials, doctors, lawyers, engineers, architects, or any other vocational group as a class.

Compensation

Money isn't everything, but enough of it is essential to enable a person to do his best work with reasonable peace of mind. And in spite of the growing emphasis on social service, there are still some people who would like enough money to enjoy the luxuries of life—a fine home, travel, boating, golf, music, paintings, antiques, rare books, or whatever. Successful accountants need not worry about obtaining whatever they consider enough.

Salary scales for accountants vary from region to region, in rough relation to the cost of living; they also vary somewhat with inflation or recession and according to supply and demand.

The demand for well-qualified college graduates with strong accounting backgrounds has exceeded the supply for twenty-five years or more, with only brief interruptions in a few recession years. Even during the recent recessionary period, good job opportunities were available to qualified accountants.

Public accounting firms and business corporations have recruited graduates most vigorously, with federal governmental agencies not far behind. The demand for able teachers of accounting at the college level is perhaps the strongest, although the recruiting effort has not been so highly organized.

Accounting firms and corporations have offered starting salaries recently as high as $12,000 to $14,000 a year to highly qualified graduates with bachelor's degrees, and from $14,000 to $18,000 to top-level applicants with master's degrees. For less highly qualified people, the scale is lower. Smaller firms and corporations, especially those outside metropolitan areas, may pay less but have some compensating advantages to offer.

Top partners in accounting firms and accounting executives in corporations frequently earn $100,000 a year and in some cases more. Down the line, an income of $25,000 to $50,000 and more is not at all uncommon. Many good people are content with less, however, in exchange for a quieter life and more leisure, which may be found in smaller organizations and in small communities.

Government and universities do not generally pay quite such high starting salaries, although they have improved greatly. The ceilings are also much lower—$30,000 to $40,000 at most. But again, both types of institutions have other satisfactions to offer. Professors, moreover, often augment their incomes with consulting work.

Choice of Work

More fascinating even than money is the wide range of work opportunities open to well-qualified accountants. They may become administrators, directing large staffs engaged in various aspects of the broad accounting function and coordinating their efforts; they may become auditors, consultants, researchers, teachers, or general practitioners.

In any of these capacities accountants may work within any one of a variety of institutions; for example, large or small corporations, large or small public accounting firms, governmental agencies of different kinds, universities, and nonprofit associations such as hospitals, foundations, and others.

Accountants can specialize in any phase of accounting of particular interest. As an auditor, an accountant may become expert in specific industries, such as oil companies, utilities, banks, brokerage firms, insurance companies, hotels, farms, and many others which have unique problems.

As a consultant, an accountant may choose income taxes as a specialty field, one which presents never-ending problems. Or specialization may be in one or more aspects of managerial accounting, such as budgeting, cost analysis, financial management, systems, or decision-making models.

Many large organizations and most universities require research in various aspects of accounting, which appeals to some individuals.

In a corporation the accountant may strive to become

chief executive officer. Scores of accountants have become officers or presidents of some of the largest companies. In government, similarly, an accountant may strive to head an agency staff. College professors may become deans or even university presidents. General practitioners are their own bosses and deal with a variety of problems facing a variety of clients.

These few paragraphs barely suggest the multiplicity of opportunities available to well-qualified professional accountants. A complete description of everything accountants do would fill another book. But a condensed review of services actually rendered by accountants may be helpful.

Independent audits, leading to professional opinions on the financial reports under examination, by definition must be conducted by independent public accountants not employees of the organizations concerned. With this exception, all other accounting activities may be conducted either by internal auditors or accountants or by public accountants on a consulting basis.

It should be borne in mind that the role of the accountant is to provide *information*, based on reliable data, which is relevant to the problem in hand. Accountants may point out alternative solutions or give advice, but they do not usurp management's responsibility for final decisions. Of course, when acting as independent auditors, accountants take sole responsibility for their own reports and opinions.

Nor do accountants develop their information and conclusions in solitude. They work closely with management and its staff and frequently with consultants from other disciplines—lawyers, bankers, engineers, insurance experts, actuaries, mathematicians, statisticians, computer experts, personnel experts, public opinion consultants, economists, behavioral scientists, or any others who can contribute useful data or help in making the resulting information as relevant to the problem as possible. The interdisciplinary approach is increasing rapidly.

The following examples of specific areas in which accountants are working may give the reader a better understanding of the choices of work available to the professional accountant.

Fields of Accounting

Auditing

Independent audits of financial reports for stockholders, creditors, the Securities and Exchange Commission, and various governmental agencies.

Cost certification for certain governmental agencies.

Compliance reports to certain governmental agencies.

Audits of municipalities and other local governmental agencies or units required by state law.

Contractors' prequalification reports to state highway departments (showing financial responsibility).

Operational audits (involving not only financial results but also the effectiveness of organizations, procedures, and personnel).

Reports to credit-rating bureaus.

Special reports on organizations that may be acquired by employer or client.

Special audits to discover suspected irregularities or the extent of fraud that has already been uncovered.

Taxation

Preparing or reviewing income tax returns.

Conferring with revenue agents on questioned items.

Planning transactions to avoid unnecessary tax liability.

Assuring compliance with various federal, state, and local tax requirements—payroll taxes, sales, property, franchise, capital stock, and other business taxes.

Estate planning.

Planning, Control, and Decision Making

Selecting methods of financing (raising capital); for example, issuing stocks or bonds, borrowing from banks or other sources (including governmental agencies in certain cases), field warehousing of inventories, discounting accounts receivable, etc.

Budgeting for operations, cash flow, capital investments.

Cost accounting for various purposes, including allocation of overhead, product-line decisions, determination of effectiveness of cost centers (performance evaluation).

Designing and installing systems for internal control, inventory control, costs control, production control, credit management, work flow, materials handling, mechanized or computerized data processing, and information systems for management at all levels.

Performing special studies, such as "make or buy" analysis, adequacy of insurance coverage, personnel compensation and incentives, product pricing, return on investment, sales forecasting, revaluation of capital assets, and, in the incipient stage, cost-benefit studies of nonprofit organizations and governmental programs.

Competition

Accountants have no exclusive privilege to develop information in these areas except in the one field of independent audits. While accountants at present are widely involved in other types of activities, so are a number of other specialists. Only by constantly updating their knowledge and skills and by superior performance can accountants expand or even maintain the scope of their services.

For example, many lawyers have acquired knowledge of accounting and specialize in tax work. When tax controversies reach the courts, only lawyers can represent taxpayers. Management consulting firms conduct special studies of many of the types indicated earlier, and some will undertake systems design and installation. Engineers and appraisers also undertake some of the functions mentioned.

Corporation employees, not trained as accountants but often holding master's degrees from graduate schools of business, have moved into key positions that might well be occupied by accountants. These MBAs have some accounting background and also may be well versed in computer technology, the systems approach to business problems, the design of mathematical decision models, and the basic concepts of comprehensive information systems.

It is indeed an open question whether the information

systems of the future will be under the control of accountants or this new breed of experts. In the past the information system was largely financial and was normally in the charge of a controller or financial vice president trained in accounting. Now, however, the trend is toward computerized information systems containing many types of nonfinancial data useful for managerial decision making. In some instances, the new kind of expert has gained control of this vital function, and the accountant-controller has been relegated to the limited area of financial reporting.

The response of the accounting profession has been to urge a broader educational base for professional accountants and to establish continuing education programs for its members, so that they will be at least as well equipped as any other group to specialize in any phase of the widening field of managerial information.

People

In any capacity they choose to work, professional accountants deal constantly with people. When employed by a single organization, they are part of a team and must work with superiors, colleagues, and subordinates. In public accounting practice they work closely with a number of different clients with various problems as well as with their own firm's partners and staff. In the universities they work with students, faculty colleagues, and administrators. Even accountants engaged in full-time research have to confer with others and report to someone.

The ancient image of the accountant seated in isolation on a high stool, wearing a green eyeshade, and entering numbers in a massive ledger is hopelessly obsolete.

Clearly, professional accountants need much more than technical knowledge and skill. They must be articulate to communicate effectively with others. They must be not only cooperative and diplomatic but also courageous enough to stand ground when necessary. Accounting is no stranger to conflict. Empathy and persuasiveness are great assets.

Accountants should be perceptive, imaginative, and able to see a problem as a whole despite, perhaps, working only on a part. They should be able to envisage many possible future consequences of current actions. They should try to put themselves in the place of those who rely on their reports or their advice, which should be made as understandable as possible.

Basically accounting is the development and communication of information to be used by people. Professional accountants, accordingly, are highly people oriented.

Summary

It has been said that when some leader in the petroleum industry developed the concept that an oil company was not merely in the oil business but in the *energy* business, new horizons opened up and new opportunities appeared.

It has also been said that if more railroad executives had conceived that they were not merely in the railroad business but in the *transportation* business, they might have been more effective competitors and avoided some of the troubles that have befallen them.

The accounting profession has recognized that it is not merely in the financial statement business but in the *information* business, which happens to be one of the most rapidly growing fields of human activity. While this may be dismissed as playing with words, words do reflect ideas, and ideas can stimulate and enlarge the creative imagination.

This book has attempted to convey the idea of a rapidly growing, rapidly expanding accounting profession, engulfed in a changing environment but determined to adapt and adjust.

The reader will have learned that accountants attained their position as professionals in a comparatively short time and that they are headed for a challenging future.

Their early preoccupation with financial reporting was a response to immediate outside pressures. So was their later involvement in income taxation. Still later, their participation in managerial accounting was stimulated by the increasing intensity of competition in American business and industry.

Now it is realized that all these areas are, as lawyers say of the law, a "seamless web." To change the metaphor, the parts are interchangeable. Accounting, broadly, can only be described as a part of an information system essential for the effective management of organizations, for internal planning, control, and decision making; and for discharging accountability to those to whom organizations have responsibility.

Quite naturally, then, as the public sector of the economy assumes increasing importance, accountants are led into social accounting—the development of information essential for the effective management of resources for social goals.

Government and nonprofit organizations—universities, hospitals, charitable organizations, membership associations and all the rest—are going to have to manage their resources more efficiently and to give a better accounting of the results of their activities.

Taxpayers, contributors, tuition fee and dues payers, who supply the resources for nonprofit organizations, are entitled to demand efficient management and full accountability, just as stockholders, creditors, and government have already demanded them of business corporations.

Yet, while new and challenging areas of service open to accountants, the more familiar ones cannot be neglected. Corporate financial reporting is far from perfect. Only a good beginning has been made in spelling out generally accepted accounting principles. Auditing techniques are in a state of transition, and unifying concepts of managerial accounting have yet to be developed.

There is much work for accountants to do in the years and decades ahead. Their efforts will, no doubt, be attended by conflict, frustration, false starts, and all the confusions endemic to democracy. But this need not be discouraging. It has always been so. Yet, if one compares the situation today with that existing even twenty-five years ago, or with that of any other nation in the world, the wonder will be that in spite of all the difficulties so much progress has been made.

Discussion Questions

1   What are some fields of specialization in accounting?
2   What are some of the advantages and disadvantages of careers in professional accounting?

3   What does the excellent compensation rate for accountants indicate about the profession?

4   What is meant in the chapter summary by the statement that "accountants are not merely in the financial statement business but in the *information* business"?

Answers to Discussion Questions

Chapter 1
What Is Accounting?

1   The primary purpose of accounting is to provide accurate and relevant information to various users (for example, investors, managements, and stockholders) to assist them in making economic decisions.

2   Accounting contributes to the welfare of society by providing information upon which economic decisions may be based. To the extent that the decisions based on quantitative information are better than they otherwise would be, accounting has assisted in a more efficient allocation of resources, which in turn provides an increased standard of living for all members of society.

3   Knowledge of accounting allows nonaccountants to communicate and understand economic terminology better, to develop an understanding of the business world and everyday business activities, and to make more informed investment and other business decisions.

4   To an investor, the role of accounting is that of reporting information, which is primarily intended for external users in order to assist them in their judgment of the company's financial position and results of operations. Management views the accounting role as that of an information source that can provide internal decision-making information. Also, management recognizes the

accounting functions of properly keeping track of company assets, helping to allocate company resources, and furnishing the management of the company with progress reports concerning the accomplishment of company objectives.

5 Several factors have contributed to the recent development of accounting. Among them are: (1) industrialization, which has increased the number of large corporations and consequently their greater need for internal and external accounting services; (2) the rapid growth in the use of accounting principles in nonprofit organizations; (3) the increase in the size of government and its resulting need to appropriate funds; (4) technological advances, for example, the computer, and their impact on accounting systems; and, (5) a greater need to allocate resources and use them more efficiently.

Chapter 2
Evolution of Accounting

1 The invention of double-entry bookkeeping was important because it enabled businesses to keep a complete and coordinated record of all transactions. Also, financial statements could be prepared at any time from the records.

2 With the Industrial Revolution came a need for large amounts of plant and equipment. Since few people could afford to buy such capital on their own, there was a need for the pooling of money. This was accomplished by forming corporations comprised of numerous shareholders. This in turn led to the subsequent need for reporting on the stewardship of the management of the corporations.

3 The role of accounting increased with the emergence of the corporations because owners were no longer managers. The separation of ownership and management functions created a need to report to the owners concerning

the progress of the corporation and the stewardship of the managers. This necessitated more accurate and more extensive accounting information. As the need for capital grew, new investors were required. Accounting had to serve the needs of these new investors. Finally, the greater size of firms requires greater internal control, planning, and decision-making processes, all of which are serviced by accounting.

4   With the development of scientific management, greater accounting skills were required because more detailed and more precise information was needed, as well as a wider range of information. Accounting not only had to serve the internal needs of planning, control, and decision making, but also the needs of outside owners and investors. Finally, greater competition meant smaller profit margins and hence a need for closer control of costs and profits by accountants and business executives.

5   As government increases in size and complexity, more funds need to be allocated and more organizations are established to administer the allocation of those funds, thereby increasing accounting services. Changes and expansions of tax and other laws also increase the demand for more accountants.

6   A primary difference between a business enterprise and nonprofit organization is the overall objective of the enterprise. The profit-seeking organization uses accounting data to plan and control for costs with the objective of making a profit. A nonprofit organization's primary goal is to allocate resources efficiently for the intended purposes of that organization. The goal is not to make a profit, but accounting data are still needed to evaluate organizational performance.

Chapter 3
Impact of Business Activity upon Accounting

1   Accounting's role in the operating cycle is unique in that it ties all functional areas together, since it must

gather information on each activity and report it to others. Also, this reporting includes determining the results or success of all other business functions individually and collectively.

2   A major factor influencing accounting methodology and practice is the influence the different user groups bring to bear upon accounting requirements. That is, various user groups, such as investors, managers, and government, have differing needs. Accounting must be sensitive to serving these needs. Thus the accounting system must necessarily gather a wide range of information as well as report relevant data to the respective groups to which it applies. The needs of different groups complicate, as well as broaden, the accountant's responsibilities.

3   The Securities and Exchange Commission has statutory authority to set accounting principles for all firms filing forms with the SEC. Traditionally, however, the SEC has allowed the accounting profession to develop generally accepted accounting principles. Nevertheless, the accounting profession must be responsive to the pressure brought to bear by the SEC or run the risk of having principles set for it by this government agency.

4   Several factors were involved in the reorganization of the primary standard-setting body within the accounting profession. Among them were: (1) the Accounting Principles Board was a volunteer organization consisting of members who were not full-time employees, and who were not able to act as quickly as was needed. (2) The APB did not have broad representation from all segments of the business community; it was comprised primarily of accountants. (3) The Financial Accounting Standards Board was established to correct some of these difficulties. It is comprised of seven full-time members who have no independent interests other than the FASB. The representation is also much broader in that all segments of the financial community are represented on the FASB. (4) The due process system of the FASB also broadens participation on important accounting matters and, therefore, makes pronouncements more acceptable by a wider segment of the financial community.

Chapter 4
Financial Reporting

1   Assets are the resources of a firm used to produce a product or service. They include cash, accounts receivable, inventory, buildings, land—all tangible as well as intangible resources having value. When an asset's benefit is exhausted, it becomes an expense.

2   Owners' equity represents stockholders' claims on the assets of a firm. The creditors' claims are reflected in the liabilities. The liabilities together with the owners' equity equal the total of the assets.

3   Interest has shifted from the balance sheet to the income statement because investors are more interested in a firm's future earning ability (as reflected in income statements) than in their current ownership claim. Creditors to a lesser degree feel the same because it is the future earnings that will be used to repay the debts of the entity.

4   Judgments and resulting estimates are required in accounting because the values of many assets cannot be known for certain, and the exact point of realization of revenues is not always determinable. Other estimates are required in terms of cost allocations.

5   The matching of revenues and expenses complicates accounting because revenues may be collected at a time different from the time when the related expense is incurred. This necessitates the use of accrual accounting techniques. However, it also provides a more meaningful measure of operating success.

6   The primary weakness of a cash basis accounting system is that it fails to match revenues and expenses and, therefore, fails to show a realistic measure of income.

Chapter 5
Auditing

1   Auditing is an investigative process incorporating analysis, testing, and checking of records as a basis for a professional opinion concerning the financial statements

of an organization. An audit deals with evidence and judgments relating to the reliability of that evidence. It adds credibility to the representations made by management in the financial statements.

2   Auditors play a unique role in attesting to financial statements in that they are paid for services rendered to management, and yet are providing an independent attestation concerning management's representations for independent third parties. This is quite different from the professional advocacy role played by the attorney, or the doctor-patient role in medicine. The accountant is providing a service to external users, but is being paid for conducting the audit by the organization whose records are being audited.

3   Auditing is preventive in that it helps detect errors in the accounting system and internal controls and thus is a deterrent to fraud and manipulation. It also helps prevent obsolescence in the accounting system and the operative internal controls.

4   Basically the independent and internal auditors perform similar tasks of checking internal control and the accounting system. However, the independent auditor also will use and verify the internal auditor's work. Independent auditors are more concerned with the verification of the company's statements in terms of fairness, while the internal auditors are primarily concerned with making sure the system is free of error and is running efficiently.

5   It is fair to hold auditors legally liable if they have been negligent in following generally accepted auditing standards or in their auditing procedures, for example, in sampling procedures. If auditors do not maintain the standards defined by the profession, they can be held liable. There is even some evidence to suggest that accountants will be held liable in the future, even if they have maintained the standards of the profession, if the financial statements upon which an opinion has been issued are not deemed to include full and fair disclosure and to fairly represent the financial condition of a company.

6   Computers have reduced the extent of routine, clerical
     work performed by auditors. They also allow the proc-
     essing of data and information to be made much more
     rapidly and efficiently. On the other hand, the computer
     has made the auditor's work more complex because in-
     formation is stored on tapes and other media that cannot
     be tested as readily. The auditor needs to know how to
     get access on a random basis to the information stored
     in computers by modern techniques. The threat of com-
     puter fraud and manipulation is also increased, which
     makes the auditor's job more complex, and requires ad-
     ditional knowledge of the computer.

7   Extension of the attest function is being mentioned by
     some in the following areas: auditing, or at least review-
     ing, interim quarterly reports of corporations; checking
     compliance with regulatory agency requirements; attest-
     ing to the reliability of systems of internal control; re-
     porting on standards for costs involved in environmental
     measures; and finally, attesting to management's effi-
     ciencies in running a company.

Chapter 6
Managerial Accounting

1   Accountants have become important members of the
     management decision-making team because they are able
     to analyze, interpret, and communicate the data they
     collect in light of the company's competitive environ-
     ment and operations. Thus they are able to contribute
     significantly to the decision-making process.

2   Cost accounting is really a part of managerial account-
     ing. Cost accounting deals with identifying, observing,
     and controlling costs. Managerial accounting takes the
     cost data, analyzes it, interprets it, and uses this infor-
     mation in the planning and budgeting processes and for
     other management decisions.

3   Variable costs are those which fluctuate with the volume
     of production. For example, if a machine is used eight

hours instead of four during the day, it naturally uses more power. As production goes up or down, so does the power bill. If, however, the machine were run all eight hours regardless of the level of production, then the power cost would be fixed because it would never change, even though production did. An example of a fixed cost is the taxes on a building. These are likely to be assessed on a basis of property values and generally have no relationship to the production schedule within a plant. It is easy to see that many, if not most, costs have both fixed and variable elements.

4   A budget is simply an estimate, a projection of what is expected to happen in the future. It is based on experience, on all relevant information, and on the best judgments available. The budget provides a tool for determining if costs are in line with expectations. If not, steps can be taken to determine why there is a variation between what was expected and what is actually occurring, and perhaps measures can be instituted to control the costs in the particular situation.

5   Standard costs are estimates or guidelines of what the actual costs should be if a firm is run efficiently. Standard costs are often used to make up a budget. They become the components of a budget for each time period or process, the budget being the summation for the entire organization. Actual costs may then be compared with the standard to see if there are variations which should be corrected.

6   A nonprofit organization will use a budget as a means of allocating its funds among the various departments and making sure that each department stays within its limits. In a profit-making organization the budget is used to determine if costs are under control so that profits can be maintained.

7   Behavioral science relates to managerial accounting because the functions of planning and control are people oriented. Costs can be controlled only by actions of people. Accountants must be aware of the impact of budgets and other cost-control techniques upon people's attitudes and, therefore, upon their actions. It is only

in fairly recent times that behavioral considerations have been stressed in managerial accounting, and it is deservedly becoming a much more important area.

8   Operations research is a term used to describe some of the newer quantitative tools being applied to business situations. It includes such areas as linear programming, PERT, CPM analysis, matrix analysis, and transportation models of various kinds. Increasingly, these tools are being utilized more extensively in the planning and control functions. Therefore they impact on accounting—especially managerial accounting, which is directly concerned with planning and control. Accountants need not be experts in operations research techniques, but they should be somewhat familiar with them.

Chapter 7
Income Tax Accounting

1   Taxable income is a measure derived by following Internal Revenue Service regulations. Accounting income is a measure derived by following generally accepted accounting principles. They are different because their purposes are different. Taxes are assessed to collect revenue for governments. From an accounting standpoint, income measures the results of operations of a business entity. IRS rules are concerned more with collectibility, while accounting income is concerned with proper matching of revenues and expenses.

2   The taxes paid over the life of an asset are the same under accelerated or straight-line depreciation, since the same amount is charged to expense over the life of the asset. However, by using accelerated depreciation, there will be less tax paid at first, with a corresponding greater amount paid during the later years of the asset's life. From a tax standpoint, this is beneficial to the firm because it receives the use of the money earlier.

3   Income tax laws provide the basis for the filing of certain information with an important regulatory agency

of the government. Because they have to comply with these laws, many companies will then use the same accounting information for their financial reporting purposes, even though in some instances it is not good accounting practice to do so. Thus it is necessary to keep two sets of books if financial reporting is to be maintained on a basis other than for tax purposes.

4   It is very difficult to write laws that are simple and yet take into consideration, on an equitable basis, all the individual circumstances and problems of, the thousands of people in the United States.

5   Tax evasion is an illegal action whereby an individual breaks the laws of the land in not paying income taxes as prescribed by the Internal Revenue Service Code and Regulations. Tax avoidance is a legal action in which an individual tries to minimize the amount of taxes which must legally be paid, based upon the IRS rules and regulations in existence at that time.

Chapter 8
Attaining Professional Status

1   Accounting is deemed a profession because (1) it renders essential services to society and recognizes a social obligation; (2) it is governed by a code of ethical conduct that is enforced by disciplinary machinery of the profession; (3) it has formal requirements for admission of new members and an identifying title that only members are permitted to use; (4) it has members who have acquired a body of specialized knowledge through a system of formal education and training; and, (5) it is recognized by law.

2   Auditing forced professional accounting standards into being because with the audit function, the accountant serves an outside interest (investors, creditors, stockholders), whereas previously, the accountant had served primarily internal management needs and, in that context, professional standards were not as necessary.

3   The development of a code of ethics is vital to accountants (1) to assist them in being recognized as a profession, (2) to gain the confidence of people, (3) to enable the discipline of accounting to be internally policed, and (4) to help accountants avoid legal liability problems now facing all professions.

4   As auditing has grown, so has the need for management consulting by public accounting firms. Because of the overall and deep understanding an accountant attains during the auditing process, management advisory services are becoming a more significant part of the accounting responsibility. Auditing, however, remains the primary function provided by the public accounting profession.

5   There has been a shift in accounting education from emphasis upon practical apprenticeship-type learning to a more formal, theoretical approach, where concepts and principles are taught in accounting programs at major universities. Some states have even gone on record stating that in the future they will require five years of formal education before an individual may sit for the CPA examination.

6   There appears to be a movement toward five-year programs in accounting. There is also a definite shift toward continuous educational requirements to retain certification. The future may also see the establishment of free-standing professional schools of accountancy, much like law schools or medical schools. There also appears to be a movement toward more detailed specialization in the various areas of accounting, such as taxation or management advisory services.

Chapter 9
Outlook for the Future

1   Some of the many possibile future developments in the field of financial reporting are: (1) the changing requirements for the capitalization of leases; (2) the disclosure of profit data by segments of companies; (3) increased

disclosure requirements for pensions; (4) reporting and auditing of forecasts of institutions; (5) continuous auditing, or at least the auditing of interim statements; (6) reporting the price-level-adjusted statements; (7) reporting current values in financial statements; and (8) reporting environmental and other social cost measures.

2   It is difficult to classify expenditures for research, advertising, and other similar items as expenses or as assets because it is difficult to measure if and when the benefits of such costs are realized. For example, is advertising an expense now, or should the related cost be deferred and spread over a period of time in which it is estimated that the revenues and the benefits will be received from that advertising?

3   Arguments favoring a greater variety of accounting reports that cover a wider range of needs include the following: (1) Accounting serves people; if the needs of these people dictate more reports covering different and more specific areas, then they should be supplied. (2) The new trends in management of personnel, social welfare, and environmental impact have created a demand for more reports covering a wider range of activities. (3) As managements' needs for information become more numerous and specific, there will undoubtedly be a need for more specific reports. (4) Government and social organizations also will feel the need for more specific reports.

4   A cost-benefit analysis of social programs is difficult primarily because the benefit side cannot easily be determined. It is fairly easy to measure the costs of a particular social program, but much more difficult to assess the timing and amount of benefits derived.

5   Human assets are the least accounted for because they are hard to judge and to measure in terms of dollars. It is difficult to assess personnel effectiveness and, since people run companies, they are not especially anxious to have other people audit or account for their performance. Also, organizational and human behaviors are fairly new areas of study, and will require a considerable amount of refinement before they can be measured accurately.

6   Accounting is a part of an information system. It is
       directed toward user needs. As the business environment
       becomes more complex and expands into new areas, as
       a result of technological advances, accounting must like-
       wise keep pace, and is therefore being pushed into
       ever-expanding areas of activity.

Chapter 10
Careers in Professional Accounting

1   Among the many fields of specialization in accounting are
       taxation, managerial accounting, nonprofit accounting,
       financial accounting with an industrial organization, pub-
       lic accounting, and the management advisory service area.

2   Some of the advantages of professional accounting careers
       are: (1) generally favorable employment opportunities,
       (2) higher-than-average compensation, (3) prestige
       that comes from being associated with a profession,
       (4) the opportunity to work closely with people, and
       (5) the challenge of working in a continually changing
       business environment. Some of the disadvantages of
       professional accounting careers include: (1) the respon-
       sibilities associated with a profession, that is, the pos-
       sibility of legal liability, and (2) the necessity to work
       long hours and to maintain currency in one profession.

3   The excellent compensation rate for accountants is an
       indication of the demand for the type of service render-
       ed by accountants. It is also an indication of the judg-
       ment and associated risk which are involved in the
       accounting profession.

4   Accountants are in the information business, not the
       financial statement business because financial statements
       are but one part of the accounting process. There are
       many other reports also produced by the accounting
       process. In addition, accountants are heavily involved
       in the interpretation and decision-making phases con-
       nected with information, as opposed to mere concern
       over presentation in financial statements.

Selected References

Readers wishing to pursue any of the subjects discussed in this book may find the publications listed below of special interest. There are, of course, countless excellent books, monographs, and articles dealing with the same subject matter. The ones mentioned here happen to be some with which the authors are familiar. For convenience, the references parallel the chapter headings in this book.

General

Bruns, William J., Jr., and Don T. DeCoster, eds. *Accounting and Its Behavioral Implications.* McGraw-Hill Book Company, New York, 1969.

Mueller, Gerhard G., and Charles H. Smith, eds. *Accounting—A Book of Readings.* Holt, Rinehart and Winston, Inc., New York, 1970.

Zeff, Stephen A., and Thomas F. Keller, eds. *Financial Accounting Theory I: Issues and Controversies*, 2nd ed. McGraw-Hill Book Company, New York, 1973.

Chapter 1
What Is Accounting?

Buckley, John W., and Marlene H. Buckley. *The Accounting Profession.* Melville Publishing Company, Los Angeles, Calif., 1974.

Description of the Professional Practice of Certified Public Accountants. American Institute of Certified Public Accountants, New York, 1966.

Designers of Order. American Institute of Certified Public Accountants, New York, 1971.

Nickerson, Clarence B. *Accounting Handbook for Nonaccountants.* Cahners Books, Boston, 1975.

Chapter 2
Evolution of Accounting

Burns, Thomas J., ed. *Accounting in Transition: Oral Histories of Recent U. S. Experience.* Ohio State University, College of Administrative Science, Columbus, 1971.

Carey, John L. *The Rise of the Accounting Profession, Vol. I: From Technician to Professional.* American Institute of Certified Public Accountants, New York, 1969.

Chatfield, Michael. *A History of Accounting Thought.* The Dryden Press, Inc., New York, 1974.

Edwards, James Don. *History of Public Accounting in the United States.* Michigan State University, Bureau of Business and Economic Research, School of Business Administration, East Lansing, 1960.

Haase, Paul. *Financial Executive Institute: The First Forty Years.* Financial Executives Institute, New York, 1971.

Littleton, A.C. *Accounting Evolution to 1900.* American Institute Publishing Co., New York, 1933.

Zeff, Stephen A. *The American Accounting Association: Its First Fifty Years.* Privately published, 1966.

Chapter 3
Impact of Business Activity upon Accounting

Carey, John L. *The Rise of the Accounting Profession, Vol. II: To Responsibility and Authority.* American Institute of Certified Public Accountants, New York, 1970, Chapters 1, 3, 5, and 6.

Establishing Financial Accounting Standards. Report of the

Study Group on Establishment of Accounting Principles. American Institute of Certified Public Accountants, New York, 1972.

McCullers, Levis D., and Relmond P. VanDaniker, eds. *Contemporary Business Environment: Readings in Financial Accounting.* Melville Publishing Company, Los Angeles, Calif., 1975.

Storey, Reed K. *The Search for Accounting Principles.* American Institute of Certified Public Accountants, New York, 1964.

Chapter 4
Financial Reporting

Basic Concepts and Accounting Principles Underlying Financial Statements of Business Enterprises. Accounting Principles Board Statement No. 4. American Institute of Certified Public Accountants, New York, 1970.

Burton, John C., ed. *Corporate Financial Reporting: Conflicts and Challenges.* Proceedings of Symposium on Corporate Financial Reporting. American Institute of Certified Public Accountants, New York, 1969.

Myer, John N. *Financial Statement Analysis,* 4th ed. Prentice-Hall, Inc., Englewood Cliffs, N.J., 1969.

Objectives of Financial Statements. Report of the Study Group on the Objectives of Financial Statements. American Institute of Certified Public Accountants, New York, 1973.

Sprouse, Robert T., and Robert J. Swieringa. *Essentials of Financial Statement Analysis.* Addison-Wesley Publishing Company, Reading, Mass., 1972.

Chapter 5
Auditing

Accountants International Study Group. *The Independent Auditor's Reporting Standards in Three Nations.* Garden

City Press, New York, 1969. Copies available from the American Institute of Certified Public Accountants, New York.

Bevis, Herman W. "The CPAs Attest Function in Modern Society." *The Journal of Accountancy*, February 1962.

Carey, John L. *The Rise of the Accounting Profession, Vol. II: To Responsibility and Authority.* American Institute of Certified Public Accountants, New York, 1970, Chapters 7 and 8.

Statement on Auditing Standards No. 1: A Codification of Auditing Standards and Procedures. American Institute of Certified Public Accountants, New York, 1973.

Statement of Issues: Scope and Organization of the Study of Auditor's Responsibilities. A Report of the Commission on Auditor's Responsibilities. American Institute of Certified Public Accountants, New York, 1975.

Chapter 6
Managerial Accounting

Bauer, Raymond A., and Dan H. Fenn, Jr. *The Corporate Social Audit.* The Russell Sage Foundation, New York, 1972.

Holmes, Arthur W., Robert A. Meier, and Donald F. Pabst. *Accounting for Control and Decisions.* Business Publications, Austin, Texas, 1970.

Horngren, Charles T. *Accounting for Management Control: An Introduction.* Prentice-Hall, Inc., Englewood Cliffs, N.J., 1974.

Jancura, Elise G., and Arnold H. Berger. *Computers: Auditing and Control.* Auerbach Publishers, Philadelphia, 1973.

Skousen, K. Fred, and Belverd E. Needles, Jr., eds. *Contemporary Thought in Accounting and Organizational Control.* Dickenson Publishing Company, Inc., Belmont, Calif., 1973.

Summers, Edward L. *An Introduction to Accounting for Decision Making and Control.* Richard D. Irwin, Inc., Homewood, Ill., 1974.

Chapter 7
Income Tax Accounting

Federal Income Tax Course. Commerce Clearing House, Chicago, issued annually.

Federal Tax Course. Prentice-Hall, Inc., Englewood Cliffs, N.J., issued annually.

Chapter 8
Attaining Professional Status

Carey, John L. *The Rise of the Accounting Profession.* 2 vols. American Institute of Certified Public Accountants, New York, 1972.

Causey, Denzil Y., Jr. *Duties and Liabilities of the CPA.* University of Texas at Austin, Bureau of Business Research, Austin, Texas, 1973.

Cerf, Alan R. *Professional Responsibility of Certified Public Accountants.* California CPAs Foundation for Education and Research, Palo Alto, 1970.

Restatement of the Code of Professional Ethics. American Institute of Certified Public Accountants, New York, 1972.

Roy, Robert H., and James H. MacNeill. *Horizons for a Profession.* American Institute of Certified Public Accountants, New York, 1967.

Study Group on Introductory Accounting. *A New Introduction to Accounting.* Price Waterhouse Foundation, New York, 1971.

Chapter 9
Outlook for the Future

Caplan, Edwin, and Stephen Landekich. *Human Resource Accounting: Past, Present and Future.* National Association of Accountants, New York, 1975.

Carey, John L. *The CPA Plans for the Future.* American Institute of Certified Public Accountants, New York, 1965.

Linowes, David. *The Corporate Conscience*. Hawthorne Books, Inc., New York, 1974.

Livingstone, John L., and Sanford C. Gunn. *Accounting for Social Goals*. Harper & Row, Publishers, Inc., New York, 1974.

Schiff, Mike, and Arie Y. Lewin. *Behavioral Aspects of Accounting*. Prentice-Hall, Inc., Englewood Cliffs, N.J., 1974.

Chapter 10
Careers in Professional Accounting

Up-to-date brochures on accounting careers may be obtained from the American Accounting Association, the American Institute of Certified Public Accountants, the American Society of Women Certified Public Accountants, the Federal Government Accountants Association, the Financial Executives Institute, the Institute of Internal Auditors, the National Association of Accountants, or from individual accounting firms.

X